The Midnight Court/
Cúirt an Mheán Oíche

Irish Studies

James MacKillop, *Series Editor*

Grand Opportunity: The Gaelic Revival and Irish Society, 1893–1910
TIMOTHY G. MCMAHON

Ireland in Focus: Film, Photography, and Popular Culture
EÓIN FLANNERY and MICHAEL GRIFFIN, eds.

Irish Orientalism: A Literary and Intellectual History
JOSEPH LENNON

Irish Theater in America: Essays on Irish Theatrical Diaspora
JOHN P. HARRINGTON, ed.

Joyce, Imperialism, and Postcolonialism
LEONARD ORR, ed.

*Making Ireland Irish: Tourism and National Identity
since the Irish Civil War*
ERIC G. E. ZUELOW

Memory Ireland: Volume 1: History and Modernity
OONA FRAWLEY, ed.

Modern Irish Drama: W. B. Yeats to Marina Carr, Second Edition
SANFORD STERNLICHT

*The Irish Bridget: Irish Immigrant Women in Domestic Service in America,
1840–1930*
MARGARET LYNCH-BRENNAN

The Myth of an Irish Cinema: Approaching Irish-Themed Films
MICHAEL PATRICK GILLESPIE

The Midnight Court/
Cúirt an Mheán Oíche

A CRITICAL EDITION

Brian Merriman

Translated by **David Marcus**

Edited and with an Introduction by
Brian Ó Conchubhair

SYRACUSE UNIVERSITY PRESS

Copyright © 2011 by Syracuse University Press

Syracuse, New York 13244-5290

First Edition 2011

11 12 13 14 15 16   6 5 4 3 2 1

∞ The paper used in this publication meets the minimum requirements
of the American National Standard for Information Sciences—Permanence of Paper
for Printed Library Materials, ANSI Z39.48-1992.

For a listing of books published and distributed by Syracuse University Press,
visit our Web site at SyracuseUniversityPress.syr.edu.

ISBN: 978-0-8156-3260-3

Library of Congress Cataloging-in-Publication Data

Merriman, Brian, 1747?–1805.

[Cúirt an mheán oíche. English]

The midnight court = Cúirt an mheán oíche : a critical edition /
Brian Merriman ; translated by David Marcus ; edited and with an Introduction
by Brian Ó Conchubhair. — 1st ed.

p. cm. — (Irish studies)

Includes bibliographical references and index.

ISBN 978-0-8156-3260-3 (pbk. : alk. paper) 1. Man–woman relationships—Poetry.
2. Bachelors—Poetry. 3. Ireland—Poetry. 4. Merriman, Brian, 1747?–1805.
Cúirt an mheán oíche. I. Marcus, David. II. Ó Conchubhair, Brian. III. Title.
IV. Title: Midnight court. V. Title: Cúirt an mheán oíche.

PB1398.M4C83 2011

891.6'213—dc23   2011024931

Manufactured in the United States of America

DAVID MARCUS

21 August 1924–9 May 2009

Contents

Contents

Illustrations

Acknowledgments

Shelly Barber (John J. Burns Library, Boston College), Beth Bland, Matthew Campbell (University of Sheffield), Patrick Griffin, Christopher Fox, Ita Daly, Hugh Fogarty (UCD), James W. Hamrick, David Horn (John J. Burns Library, Boston College), Ken Kenslow, Dyann Mawhorr, James MacKillop (Syracuse University Press), Alan Hayes, Brendan Kane (UConn), Sean O'Brien, Breandán Ó Buachalla (RIP), Liam Ó Peaircín (University of Limerick), and D. J. Whyte (Syracuse University Press). I am particularly grateful to Brian Ó Dálaigh for his generous assistance with place names and as ever to Chantelle Snyder, who designed the map of Clare. A final thank you to the Notre Dame undergraduates who taught me to translate the various translations into American English. Mo bhuíochas aríst eile do Thara—Is gnáth sinn ar siúl le ciumhais na habhann, ar bháinseach úr is an drúcht go trom.

Introduction

Brian Merriman's Daytime Milieu

BRIAN Ó CONCHUBHAIR

Yet I could wish that a Gaelic scholar had been found, or
failing that some man of known sobriety of manner and of
mind . . . to introduce to the Irish reading public this vital,
extravagant, immoral, preposterous poem.

—YEATS 1926, 5

I guess the best way to sum it all up is to say that I do not
suppose 99 out of a 100 American Irishmen have ever heard
of Brian Merriman. I had not myself until about five years
ago. Such a lack of awareness of something authentic, unique,
and remarkable out of one's past is just plain tragic.

—GREELEY 1980, 241

Cúirt an Mheán Oíche is a late-eighteenth-century Irish-language
poem of over one thousand lines composed by Brian Merriman
in County Clare, Ireland.[1] Considered "one of the greatest comic

---

1. Some uncertainty surrounds the orthography of the poet's name in Irish
and English. The version "Brian Merriman" has been chosen from the various
options available (Bryan Merryman, Brian Merríman, Brian Mac Giolla Meidhre,

xiii

Introduction

works of literature, and certainly the greatest comic poem ever written in Ireland," (Ó Tuama 1995, 64) it has not only entertained the general public, intrigued scholars, fascinated literary detectives, enraged puritans, and attracted translators and transcribers[2] but also shocked readers in multiple translations. Generally accepted to have been composed around 1780 in County Clare—"a part of Ireland which must have been as barbarous as any in Europe" (O'Connor 1945, 5)—its title has subsequently been rendered as *Mediae Noctis Consilium* in Latin, *Der Mitternächtige Gerichtshof* in German, *Le Tribunal de Minuit* in French, *La Noktmeza Kortumo* in Esperanto, *Cùirt a'Mheadhain Oidhche* in Scots-Gaelic, and *The Midnight Court/The Midnight Verdict/On Trial at Midnight* in English.[3] Numerous editions, versions, and interpretations have also appeared in print and on radio, stage, and television. Regardless of language or medium, however, *Cúirt an Mheán Oíche* remains today, as when first composed, "[a] poem of gargantuan energy, moving clearly and

---

Brian MacNamara, and many others) because it is the most often used in English-language scholarship and is readily recognizable. Throughout this volume the form *Cúirt an Mheán Oíche* is used rather than the various alternate spellings used at different periods which include *Cúirt an Mheadhan Oidhche, Cúirt an Mheon-Oíche, Cúirt an Mheon Oíche, Cúirt an Mheánoíche, Cúirt an Mheadhon Oídhche, Cúirt an Mheadhán Oidhche,* and *Cúirt an Mheadhon Oidhche.*

2. Ó Tuama (1995, 64) notes that "scores of copies were transcribed and reproduced in the immediate years after its composition: it was read with avidity, discussed and frequently added to."

3. Breandán Ó Buachalla has noted that early January 1780 is the decree's date of enactment, but cautions that this "date has been taken by people as the date of the composition of the poem, which it might not necessarily be. . . . [It is a] mistake to assume that because they give this date in the poem as the date of enactment of the law, that it automatically follows that that's the date of the poem. It could be twenty years earlier, it could be twenty years later—my sense is that it's earlier" (2005).

Introduction

pulsating along a simple storyline, with a beginning, a middle and an end. For a poem of over one thousand lines it has few *longeurs*"[4] (Ó Tuama 1995, 72). Despite its simple storyline, the poem touches on a multitude of themes and its subject matter retains public interest and shock value today as much as at any time since it was first unleashed. Frank O'Connor quipped that the poem contained "things which even Yeats himself might have thought twice of writing in English-speaking Dublin of the twentieth [century]" (O'Connor 1945, 9). These things include such perpetually contentious and divisive topics as clerical celibacy, concealed pregnancy, free love, illegitimacy, infidelity, casual sex, marriages between partners of disparate ages, the superiority of bastards and foundlings, promiscuity, seduction, sexual frustration, the utility of marriage as a social institution, and the social value of virginity.

Merriman lived at a time of tumultuous change and upheaval: the French revolution in Paris, the Rebellion of the United Irishmen in Ireland, and the Revolutionary War in America. In cultural terms it was a period that witnessed the publication of such foundational and influential texts as *The Wealth of Nations, Critique of Pure Reason, Introduction to the Principles of Morals, Songs of Innocence, A Vindication of the Rights of Women,* and *The Rights of Man.* In legal and constitutional terms it heralded a new constitution in the former colonies and Parliament's repeal of the Penal Laws in Ireland through the Catholic Relief Acts of 1771, 1778, and 1793. And in the sphere of social justice, it heard debates over democracy, liberty,

---

4. Discussing the nonlinear incoherence of contemporary long poems in English, critic Richard Terry depicts them as "generically polymorphous, assimilating meditative, descriptive, didactic, satiric, comic, rhapsodic, and panegyrical veins of writing. Additionally, their local rhetorical colors had a habit of being borrowed miscellaneously from elsewhere" (1992, 496).

Introduction

and egalitarianism as well as the appropriate punishment for infanticide and concealment of births in England and, in 1803, the repeal of the 1624 Act "to Prevent the Destroying and Murthering of Bastard Children" (Jackson 1996, 162). In literary terms *Cúirt an Mheán Oíche* trails *Caoineadh Airt Uí Laoire/The Lament for Art O'Leary* (1773) and predates Micheál Ó Braonáin's composition *Príomhshruth Éireann/The Principal River of Ireland* (1794) and the compositions of Antoine Ó Raifteirí/Anthony Raftery (1784–1835).[5] Despite the relevant merits of these various Irish texts, *Cúirt an Mheán Oíche* surpasses them all for coordinated power of linguistic dexterity, sheer scope of artistic achievement, vitality of imagination, and perpetual relevance and interest.[6] The verbal manipulation and

---

5. It is assumed to be contemporaneous with Donnchadha Ruadh Mac Conmara's *Eachtra Ghiolla An Amhráin/Adventures of a Luckless Fool* and Mícheál Ó Cuimín's *Laoidhe Oisín i dTír na nÓg*, but see note 3 above.

6. See Power (1990, 6). Ciarán Carson (2009) labels it "a poem of deep linguistic resource, scabrous, tragic and humorous by turns, immensely sophisticated in its verbal music. . . . There are times when there is a kind of desperation in Merriman's rhetoric and manic word-play. But the writing of *Cúirt an Mheán Oíche* would not have been possible without an audience sophisticated enough in the language to appreciate its finer points." With regard to the poem's metrics, Ó Buachalla has commented, "For a poem like this, you have no notion of understanding the efficacy of the poem or its intrinsic worth [without metrics]" (2005, n.p.). Merriman's use of rhyming couplets, a common feature of English-language verse, has led some critics, most notably Frank O'Connor, to promote Augustinian poetry as a possible influence. Once again, Ó Buachalla rebuffs such claims: "The basic structure of the poem is well attested in Irish, and well known in Irish, and used primarily for declarative verse . . . a fairly common meter, a traditional one . . . [he] embellished with the notion of the couplet. . . . Ó Rathaille himself has several examples in his laments, curiously enough, of rhyming couplets, which haven't been noticed. Merriman . . . brought certain elements of the traditional metrical . . . to an apex of perfection" (2005, n.p.).

Introduction

the sustained thematic treatment alone entitle it to the praise heaped on it by critics. It has nevertheless remained "uniquely resistant to interpretation" (Buttimer 2006, 320) and has persistently thwarted scholars' efforts to interpret it critically in any authoritative fashion.

The poem not only dispels but inverts many presumptions and assumptions about Ireland and Irish-language literature and attracts competing and conflicting critiques. Elizabeth Butler Cullingford has described it as a "literary half-breed" (1994, 172), "a parody inversion of normal legal practice, a Bakhtinian world-turned-upside-down in which women are on top. . . . Desire is sanctioned rather than restrained by the Law" (171). The text's unusual themes and frank treatment force critics to make extreme judgments, often motivated more by ideological and moral agendas than aesthetical or literary concerns. Writing in 1935, Aodh de Blacam deemed the text "indecent." Despite being "the most vigorous composition of late Gaelic poetry," it was nevertheless, he wrote, "a thing that we could lose without a sigh. The poet's mind must have been a soured and mocking mind, lacking in the gentle qualities" (1935, 139).

Consequently, scholars seek international influences as inspiration while others strive to establish the purely native origins of "this dark flower of Irish literature" (Everett-Green 2005). The possible literary influences and sources run the gamut of eighteenth-century European literature and political thought. Critics have argued and debated the merits of the medieval Courts of Love, sixteenth- and seventeenth-century English ballads, Dean Swift's *Cadenus and Vanessa*, Richard Savage's "The Bastard," and Guillaume de Lorris/Jean de Meung's *Roman de la Rose*[7] as well as the possible influence

---

7. *Roman de la Rose* is a satire on the monastic orders, celibacy, the nobility, the Papal See, the excessive pretensions of royalty, and especially on women and marriage.

Introduction

of Burns and Goldsmith, not to mention the political and philosophical tracts of Voltaire and Rousseau. Nor do all critics entertain the European thesis. Writing in *Punch* in November 1945, as the world emerged from the horrors of the war—a conflict in which the Irish Free State had elected to remain neutral—and prepared for the Nuremberg War Trials, P. M. F. (Mrs. D. J. L. Fitzgerald) expressed her surprise at the "unstinted praise, especially for his European culture, for which there is no evidence whatever," lavished on Merriman by his Irish admirers (407). Rather, the poem is a "rollicking, spirited and slangy poem in Irish Gaelic . . . [but] the student of literature will realize at once that it is the old stock 'dream debate' of fourteenth-century poetry, and that the people in it (*le jaloux, la mal mariée,* the priest and the maiden) are the stock medieval characters; the only wonder is that Merriman, writing in 1780, could have produced such a gay, spirited and colloquial poem in a form which was already about forty years out of date" (406–7).

The pursuit of possible influences has dogged *Cúirt an Mheán Oíche* since it was first translated and perhaps before.[8] Ó Tuama captured the enduring frustration at this never-ending game pursued by literary sleuths as follows: "Or, or, or . . . the permutations of the possibilities seem endless" (1995, 71). The pertinent unanswered question remains—to what extent, if any, did Merriman avail himself of various strands of political thought, social theories, and literary texts when composing *Cúirt an Mheán Oíche*? Had Merriman, "teaching school in a God-forsaken village" (O'Connor 1945,

---

8. While most attention has focused on possible sources for Merriman's poem, W. J. McCormack (1994, 265) posits *Cúirt An Mheán Oíche* as a possible comparison with the "Circe" episode of James Joyce's novel *Ulysses*. See also Heffernan (2004), Maria Tymoczko (1994, 196–202), and Martin J. Croghan (1995, 19–30).

Introduction

9) access to, and awareness of, these various movements, debates, and texts? What elements, if any, filtered through his consciousness and imagination to emerge in an altered state in his poem, in his characters' speeches, or in the court's final verdict? Or do critics, as J. E. Caerwyn Williams and Máirín Ní Mhuiríosa suggest, stress the text's "novelty" at the expense of native sources?[9] (1979, 300). Breandán Ó Buachalla, the foremost scholar of eighteenth-century Ireland, rejected the notion that such innovations as might be in the text had to be attributed to external factors alone. He dismissed such "geographical determinism that a person from Clare could not write poetry or that for a certain type of poetry you need a certain type of hinterland." He equally set aside the view that "the Irish literary tradition could not produce a work like this; it could, and it did, and it is still capable of doing so. Because that's another aspect of some of the commentary, that this was a dying tradition, and it is amazing that a dying tradition could produce two poems like *Caoine Airt Uí Laoire* and *Cúirt an Mheon-Oíche* as it was gasping! It wasn't gasping; it was a vibrant tradition, and a vibrant literary tradition, which could produce major works of creativity, which this is" (Ó Buachalla 2005, n.p.).[10] More recently, Gearóid

9. "An amhlaidh a chuireann roinnt léirmheastóirí strus ró-mhór ar 'úire' smaointe Bhriain Merriman? Is fíor go raibh smaointe úra 'san aer' ar fud na hEorpa sa dara leath den 18ú haois agus is fíor nár ró-dheacair do dhuine mar Bhrian eolas a chur ar na tuairimí réabhlóideacha a bhí á nochtadh ag údair mar Voltaire agus Rousseau. Ach an gá dul chomh fada sin ó bhaile chun foinsí cuid de smaointe Bhriain a lorg? Nach bhfuil seans ann gur i mbéaloideas na ndaoine a bhí cuid de na foinsí sin?" (Caerwyn Williams and Ní Mhuiríosa 1979, 300).

10. Ó Buachalla identified the decline in population motif as the text's only innovative development. "All the others—the notion of a young girl, an old man, of marriage—all those, they abound, particularly in Irish folk songs. . . . In French

Introduction

Ó Crualaoich has emphasized the text's originality and innovativeness within the native tradition. He argues that a decade before the proliferation of female allegorical representations in postrevolution France, Merriman "achieved a revolutionary reinterpretation of the Irish sovereignty queen myth that made a profound mark on vernacular culture here . . . [and] produced a poem which brings one of the deepest myths of Irish culture (learned and vernacular) to bear in an imaginatively creative and extremely novel way on issues arising from the contemporary social and political context" (2003, 67). Merriman's concern throughout the poem, Ó Crualaoich contends, is with "the flowering of human sexuality and while this, in itself, is not a radical departure in literature, what is startling in the Irish literary tradition is the informing of the call with the power and authority of the Gaelic sovereignty myth whose bona fide, or wit, in Ireland, runs back to insular Celtic times." In an important intervention, Ó Crualaoich distinguishes between the majority of the *aisling* poets who sought a political reconfiguration, and Merriman's desired outcome, which is "truly revolutionary, in that he invokes its characters, its images and its power not only in the cause of tribal, dynastic or national sovereignty, but in the cause of civil and psychological liberation of the individual at the personal level" (2003, 68). This era in County Clare, as Pádraig Ó Fiannachta

---

political literature, the notion that France is decaying is pervasive, and then as the century moves on, before the revolution, it's linked with anti-Catholicism and that one of the remedies for the falling population of France is for priests to marry" (2005, n.p.). Kevin Whelan has demonstrated that the link between a nation's demography and its power was a basic eighteenth-century assumption. The negative connotation of Ireland as an overpopulated country is a much later phenomenon. The depiction of Ireland as an underpopulated country is present in Arthur Young's *Tour in Ireland* (1780).

Introduction

documents, furnished Merriman and his fellow intellectuals with a vibrant Irish-language literary discourse (Ó Fiannachta 1982, 229–46; Ó Cuív 1986, 391). *Cúirteanna filíochta*/poetic courts served as social and literary networks for scribes, poets, and oral intellectuals and provided forums where they discussed, debated, and bettered one another's arguments and opinions. Liam P. Ó Murchú's groundbreaking study *Merriman: I bhFábhar Béithe* traces Merriman's possible connections with the Thomond and Munster literary circles (2005, 10). In addition to identifying Tomás Ó Míocháin, Séamas Mac Consaidín, Seon Lluid, Seán de Hóra, and Seán Ó Tuama an Ghrinn (Ó Murchú 2005, 51–58; Ó Muirithe 1988, 8–9) as potential key stakeholders in this literary enterprise, Ó Murchú argues convincingly for the seventeenth-century devotional poet Murchadh Riabhach Mac Namara as an important source for Merriman (2005, 20–43, 109–34).

Such questions and considerations envelop this poem and have long bewildered critics and continue to dominate the poem, at times even distracting from its imaginative power and humorous insubordination. To consider such issues is to enter several debates surrounding the poem, debates that are rarely, if ever, conclusive. Attempting answers brings to the fore the extent and speed of communication and dissemination of news, literature, and philosophy in late eighteenth-century Europe and in particular the relationship between the margins (County Clare) and metropolitan centers such as Dublin, Edinburgh, London, and Paris.

This volume has two aims: to introduce North American students to Brian Merriman's eighteenth-century poem in translation and to present the major arguments and debates surrounding it. Four essays specifically written for students with no prior knowledge of the Irish-language literary tradition discuss the cultural history that informed the poem's composition and shaped

Introduction

subsequent debates and controversies. David Marcus's English-language version offers access to the original text's themes, tone, and tenor via translation and "while he may not have remained faithful to the letter of the original, he has, nonetheless, rendered the racy spirit of Merriman as no other translator has done" (O'Flaherty 1967, 101). This particular translation is glossed wherever it was felt that cultural references or idioms may possibly be unfamiliar to American undergraduates. It is a truism that no translation ever matches its original. This axiom is especially true with regard to *Cúirt an Mheán Oíche* as so much of its power is linguistically and metrically driven, and consultation of the original is essential for any student intent on scholarly research. That should not discourage readers from approaching the poem in translation, but rather caution against rash judgments on some of the obscurities that surround it. Students intent on pursuing further reading or independent research will find a bibliography of pertinent essays and texts as well as a timeline of key political, cultural, and literary events from Merriman's lifetime. A glossary of terms is also provided, as is a list of the text's various publications, translations, adaptations, and presentations. A map identifies important sites in Merriman's life and locations mentioned in the text. Space and copyright issues do not permit a dual-language edition. This absence is lamentable for many reasons, not least because whatever the future shall reveal of its sources, inspirations, or motivations, the principal glory of *Cúirt an Mheán Oíche* remains its language (O'Rahilly 1912, 203). While the original text is available in various manuscripts, Liam P. Ó Murchú's scholarly edition *Cúirt an Mheon-Oíche le Brian Merríman* is essential for any serious student of the poem, and the Irish-language quotations are from that edition. The reader approaching the text via translation loses much, mostly in terms of the poem's language and verbal adroitness but also the wit and

Introduction

humor that abounds throughout.[11] Nonetheless, Ó Tuama noted: "*The Midnight Court* can, of course, be read with immense enjoyment and profit by a reader who has no knowledge whatever of its literary background and antecedents" (1995, 72). The four essays, written by scholars experienced in teaching *Cúirt an Mheán Oíche* in translation to North American students, contextualize the text and critique the major scholarly approaches to it. Alan Titley sets out to explain why the poem continues to attract readers, scholars, and translators two hundred years after the poet's death. He carefully leads the reader through the poem's prologue, three dramatic monologues, and epilogue while demonstrating the links to the native tradition and identifying common literary forms and motifs. He discusses and dismisses various interpretations, including those that read the poem as social realism or as an unresolved moral dilemma, as well as those critics who use Merriman to promote their own cultural, social, or literary agendas. Among the latter is Frank O'Connor, whose English-language translation was controversially banned in 1945. That O'Connor's translation was proscribed is hardly surprising given that contemporary Catholic theologians considered "[t]he theme of virginity is allied to whatever is deepest in the human heart, and it lies also at the centre of the Catholic Church. To write about it is like making a joyous inventory of what is, in our own day as well as in the first centuries of Christianity, one of the richest treasure hoards of Christian virtue" (Perrin 1956, vii). Nor was this instance of censorship

11. For explanations by various translators on their individual approach see Marcus (1989). See also O'Connor (1945, 7); Power (1990, 7–8); Carson (2005, 11). While written in 1953, Marcus's translation retains its contemporary vernacular value and those difficulties that arise are due more to the difference between standard American English, Hiberno-English, and standard British English.

Introduction

unique. To much less fanfare in 1949, Lord Longford's printer also demanded the removal of several lines from his translation, and theatrical productions have also attracted controversy.[12]

If Titley sees little new, original, or surprising other than how the poet deploys his material, Michael Griffin depicts Merriman living, working, and writing at the cusp of two distinct literary discourses in eighteenth-century County Clare. Drawing on the work of Declan Kiberd, Liam de Paor (1988; 1998), and Pádraig Ó Fiannachta, he examines the bilingual literary culture of Clare and explores the libertarian and libertine currents that pervade the poem and provide its political and social charge. Merriman, in Griffin's view, occupies an isthmus between two cultures having recourse to an Irish and an English-language literary discourse. Considering the emerging print culture in County Clare during Merriman's lifetime, he calls, in conclusion, for a modification of Ó Tuama's rejection of the European Enlightenment in favor of late medieval inspiration encapsulating Merriman's own indigenous culture. In addition, he urges critics to consider a vernacular enlightenment, more diverse and complex than the standard print culture enlightenment.

Sarah McKibben, in the third essay, considers the text's multi-directional mockery and focuses critical attention on issues of gender, in particular how gendered discourse functions in the poem. This skillful reading exposes the reader to the literary history of eighteenth-century Irish-language literature and demonstrates how

12. See correspondence regarding the propriety of performing a dramatized version of the play on Good Friday in the *Irish Times*, 1, 5, and 15 Apr. 1996. See also Ó Glaisne (1996). See also Kenrick (1794) for late-eighteenth-century attitudes toward virginity.

Introduction

Merriman simultaneously mimics and manipulates other genres, ideological constructs, and the various gender constructions they entail. McKibben advances the argument that in celebrating the bastard as superordinately healthy and virile, the text poses hybridity rather than purity as a source of cultural, literary-linguistic, and communal strength.

Since Aoibheall's judgment concerns reshaping public policy and attitudes, it is fitting that Bríona Nic Dhiarmada in the final essay engages with issues of popular reception and scholarly interpretation. Considering the most appropriate way for twenty-first-century readers to approach this text, she scrutinizes how past critics skewed their interpretations to suit dominant tastes. Noting that the text has retained its popularity and public appeal despite seismic shifts in language, politics, and social values, she examines how the text—both the original and translation—was framed to suit contemporary fashions. *Cúirt an Mheán Oíche* has long provoked debate, and as Nic Dhiarmada demonstrates, controversial readings show no sign of dwindling any time soon.

Whether the poem "radically articulates the feminine side of the human psyche . . . [and] demands . . . personal psychic liberation from the distortions of an excessively patriarchal social order" (Ó Crualaoich 2003, 69), or merely "challenges the hegemony of male values, male power, civil and ecclesiastical" (67) or is simply "old stock" medieval mutton dressed up as Enlightenment lamb is yet another of the several enigmas surrounding this poem. The divergent readings demonstrate the wide spectrum of opinion regarding the poem, judgments that lurch from nativist triumphalism to the European Enlightenment, from wholesome praise to damning indictment. The result is a cascade of valid questions but few revealing answers. As befits a literary text of the highest quality, the more it is probed, the more it reveals.

Introduction

Whatever the provenance of *Cúirt an Mheán Oíche*, whether native or foreign or a combination of both, it remains a remarkable production that appeals to generation after generation whether as readers, listeners, viewers, scholars, or translators. Yet despite the multiple translations, editions, reissues, and dramatizations, it appears that *Cúirt an Mheán Oíche* is constantly rediscovered.[13] This volume will be successful if it encourages a new generation of students to experience the delights offered by the poem and encourages teachers to include this fascinating and rewarding text in university and college courses. In addition to its thematic richness and technical virtuosity, an additional attraction—were one required—is the fact that "[t]here is no text, not even *Ulysses*, whose fate in the 20th century interacted with the national culture as significantly as Brian Merriman's *Cúirt an Mheán Oíche*" (Ní Chuilleanáin 2005, C13). To follow the history of this poem from manuscript to printed page, through the censorship controversy to the international stage, is to trace the path of Irish modernity. Piaras Béaslaí once proclaimed that "those who approach this work in the proper spirit will derive from it all the delight of a literary voyage" (1912, 19). That sentiment is as valid now at the conclusion of the first decade of the twenty-first century as it was at any time since *Cúirt An Mheán Oíche* was first composed. It is equally true of the never-ending scholarly concerns and contentions that beleaguer this remarkable, distinctive, and immensely agreeable Irish text.

---

13. Critics, such as Kate Kellaway (1995) in *The Observer*, describe *Cúirt an Mheán Oíche* as "an extraordinary, neglected poem written in the Irish language." Also, Alasdair Macrae (1993) claims in the *Glasgow Herald* "A poet who deserves a wider audience is Brian Merriman, whose *A Midnight Court*, written in Irish (1780), is a wildly funny ridiculing of current attitudes to sex and the Church."

Part One

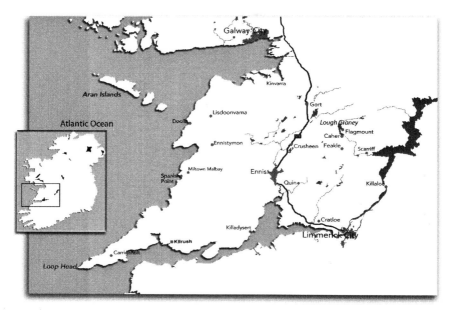

County Clare. Courtesy of Chantelle Snyder, graphic designer, University of Notre Dame.

The Midnight Court

BRIAN MERRIMAN

English Translation by DAVID MARCUS

The first part, in which the poet while savouring the pleasures of the great outdoors is forced to pay a visit to court where a pertinent case is at hearing.

Beside the water I often walk	1
Through fields where the dew is as thick as chalk;	
With the woods and the mountains just in sight	
I hang around for the dawn to light.	
Loch Graney[1] lifts my soul with joy—	5
Such land! Such country! What a sky!	
How silently the mountains rest	
Their heads upon each other's breast.	
This view would bring the heart to life—	
Be it worn with sickness, age, or strife—	10
In the poorest beggar that ever stood	
Were he but to glance beyond the wood	
At the fleet of ducks, when the mist has gone,	

---

1. *Loch Gréine* [anglicized as Lough Graney]: a lake in northeast County Clare, approximately one thousand acres in extent.

Convoyed by a single swan,
And the jumping fish that shoot and flash   15
High in the air with a rainbow splash,
The blue of the lake and the breakers' roar
Tossing and tumbling towards the shore;
Birds on the branch that whistle and sing,
Frolicking fawns that soar and spring,   20
The sound of the horn and a glimpse of the hunt
With the pack in chase and the fox in front.
Yesterday, shooting from the east,
And melting away the morning mist,
The sunrays flashed and darted by,   25
Burning a track across the sky.
The nodding branches all around,
The very grass upon the ground,
The growth so green and flowers so fair
Would soon dispel the worst despair.   30
Then, drowsy, dull and half-asleep,
I rested where the grass was deep
Along a tree-lined, shady ditch[2]
Where there was room for me to stretch.
No sooner had I closed my eyes,   35
My face being covered from the flies,
And settled for a peaceful doze
Than in my dreams the flies arose
And swarmed about me in attack
While I, asleep, could not hit back.   40

2. Ditch: an embankment or mound formed by earth thrown up when digging a trench.

Brief was my rest when, it appeared,
With shocks and shakes the mountains reared,
The north was numbed with thunder-crash,
The waves were laced with lightning-flash;
Whatever look I chanced to take   45
I saw, approaching by the lake,
A hellish, hairy, haggard hank,[3]
Bearded, bony, long and lank;
Her height I'd estimate for sure
At twenty feet, and maybe more,   50
For yards behind she dragged her coat
Through all the muck and mire and mud;
It took some nerve merely to glance
Upon that ghoulish countenance
For with her ghastly, toothless grin   55
She'd frighten the life out of anyone.
To top it all, in a mighty paw
Was the biggest staff I ever saw
And in letters of brass the information
That she had a bailiff's qualification.[4]   60
Then, with a gruff and angry shout,
"Get up!" she snarled, "You lazy lout;
A nice, bloody thing: you're stretched in state
While the Court's convened and thousands wait.
And this is no court where the law is bent   65

---

3. Hank: a participant in bull-baiting, considered a sport.

4. Bailiff's qualification, or barántas: a legal warrant, typically an arrest warrant that identifies the plaintiff and the crimes of which he or she is charged along with the time, date, and venue of the trial, but also a literary genre associated with Munster poetry. For further information see Welch 1996 and Ó Fiannachta 1978.

Like the courts of graft that you frequent,
But one that is run by the pure in heart
Where Virtue, Justice, Right take part.
It's something the Irish could put in their songs—
That it takes the best to judge their wrongs; 70
And up in Moy Graney's[5] palatial fort
For the past two nights they've been holding court.
The Chief Justice himself in particular—
And all the big-wigs[6] of the Bar[7]—
Without exception every man-jack's[8] 75
Up in arms that Ireland's bandjaxed:[9]
Farms are bankrupt, freedom banned,
No law or leader in the land;
Our country's raped and Luck, the coward,
Shuns a virgin that's deflowered— 80
Far afield our men are shipped
While by grabbing hands she's stripped
And as, powerless, we watch,
All her beauty they debauch.
But still there is the final curse— 85
Lack of redress. What could be worse

5. *Maigh Gréine* (anglicized Moy Graney): the plain overlooking Lough Graney/Loch Gréine.

6. Big-wig: humorous or contemptuous reference to a man of high official standing or importance.

7. Bar or Court of Justice: lawyers were allowed to speak beyond the bar that divided the courtroom into public spectators and the legal profession, jury, and judges.

8. Man-jack: an ordinary person.

9. Ban(d)jaxed: Battered, destroyed, or ruined.

Than seeing one you love undone
And being forced to watch the fun?
They scorn our laws and ape our cries,
Promise the world—but it's all lies;   90
Right is guyed with mocks and gibes
And hangs there—its mouth stuffed with bribes.
The Court considered the country's crisis,
And what do you think its main advice is—
That unless there's a spurt in procreation   95
We can bid goodbye to the Irish nation;
It's growing smaller year by year—
And don't pretend that's not your affair.
Between death and war and ruin and pillage
The land is like a deserted village;   100
Our best are banished, but you, you slob,
Have you ever hammered a single job?
What use are you to us, you cissy?
We have thousands of women who'd keep you busy,
With breasts like balloons or small as a bud   105
Buxom of body and hot in the blood,
Virgins or whores—whatever's your taste—
At least don't let them go to waste;
It's enough to make us broken-hearted—
Legs galore—and none of them parted.   110
They're ready and willing for any endeavour—
But you can't expect them to wait forever.
And as the Court has recommended
That all this nonsense must be ended,
A judge was chosen without delay   115
To hear what both sides have to say.

'Twas Munster's[10] friend and Craglee's[11] queen,
Aeval,[12] of heart and spirit clean,
Who has been picked to try and see
If she can find a remedy.   120
And she has solemnly sworn and vowed
That no exceptions will be allowed;
She'll stand by the poor and the weak she'll save,
And see to it that the rich behave,
She won't take long to curb the strong   125
And Right won't have to give way to Wrong.
She's an eye on the fellows who think they're smart:
No spiv[13] or pimp or painted tart

10. Munster, Leinster, Ulster, and Connaught constitute the four provinces of Ireland. Munster consists of six counties: Clare, Cork, Kerry, Limerick, Tipperary, and Waterford.

11. *Craig Liath* (anglicized as Craglee), near Killaloe. This location is associated with Aoibheall, Queen of the Munster fairies in folk-belief. See MacKillop (1998, 97).

12. Aeval (pronounced Evil): a transliteration of the Irish personal name, Aoibheall, the fairy queen and protector of the Dál gCais sept in County Clare. She is associated with Munster and Craglee in particular. "Her name meant 'sparkling' or 'bright' and reflects a common attribute of goddesses in ancient Irish culture. . . . The twelfth-century tract on King Brian Boru states that on the night before the battle of Clontarf, Aoibheall appeared to him and foretold he would be killed in that contest and that the first of his sons whom he would see on that day would succeed him as king. . . . The post-medieval poets numbered Aoibheall as one of the principal otherworld women of Munster." See Ó hÓgáin (1991, 38) and MacKillop (1998, 5). She also features in Donncha Ruadh mac Conmara's famous Irish-language poem, *Eachtra Ghiolla an Amaráin/Adventures of a Luckless Fellow,* written circa 1750.

13. Spiv: a flashily dressed man living on his wits without regular employment, having the implication of petty criminal activity.

Will treat the law as a thing of sport
While Aeval rules the Midnight Court.   130
It's assembled in Feakle[14] this very day
And she'd like to hear what you've to say,
So up with you now or else you'll find
My boot disturbing your fat behind."
Then suiting her action to her words   135
She lofted me like a sack of spuds[15]
And over the hills I was jet-propelled
Till we reached Moinmoy[16] where the Court was held.
And there, as I stood, before my sight
Was a massive mansion ablaze with light,   140
Rich and radiantly draped,
Beautifully built and shaped;
There was the Queen, looking kind and mild
As she sat on the Bench and sweetly smiled;
Hundreds of grim, gigantic guards   145
Were stationed at every couple of yards,
And, packed as tight as a sardine,
Was the biggest crowd I had ever seen.
Then there appeared a majestic maid,
Slender, silky, soft, and sad,   150
With skin as tanned as the golden sand
And she took her place on the witness-stand.
Her hair was flowing loose and free

14. *An Fhiacail* (anglicized as Feakle): a parish in northeast County Clare that forms the northeastern extremity of the county. See Ó Dálaigh (2000, 108–9).

15. Spud: a potato.

16. *Cnoic Mhánmhaí* (anglicized as Moinmoy): a series of hills in the parish of Feakle.

But her face was a picture of misery;
Her eyes were fierce and flashed with hate   155
And she'd worked herself up into such a state
That she moaned and heaved and sobbed and sighed
But couldn't speak, though hard she tried.
You could see from the flood of tears she shed
That she'd much prefer to have dropped down dead   160
Than to stand in the witness-box alone
Exposing her grief to everyone.
After a while, as her sobs grew weak,
She made a determined attempt to speak,
And finding her passion at last was spent,   165
She spoke, and this was her argument:
"O Aeval, greetings from my heart
To you, who Craglee's[17] ruler art;
Our sun by day, our moon by night,
Our only comfort and delight,   170
O strong protector, firm and true,
Munster and Ireland depend on you;
The start of my story, the source of my strain,
The reason I'm senseless and almost insane,
The thing that has taken and torn me in twain[18]   175
And has pricked me with pangs and has plagued me
        with pain—
Is the number of women, old and young,

17. *Léithchraig* (anglicized as Craglee): the reputed home of Aoibheall, the fairy queen of Munster.

18. Twain: into two parts or pieces.

For whom no wedding-bells have rung,
Who become in time mere hags and crones[19]
Without man or money to warm their bones.   180
Thousands will back my evidence,
And I speak, alas, from experience;
Like me, I can swear, there's many another
Aching to be a wife and mother,
But the way we're ignored you'd think we're wrecks   185
Possessed of gender but not of sex;
At night with longing I'm lacerated,
Alone in bed I lie frustrated
And damned with dreams of desire denied
My hunger goes unsatisfied.   190
O Aeval, you must find a way
To save our women without delay,
For if the men are allowed to shirk
We'll have to force them to do their work.
By the time they're ready to take a wife   195
They're not worth taking to save their life,
They're stiff and shrunken and worn and weak
And when they mount you they wheeze and creak.
Then if, by chance, some lusty beau
Whose beard has hardly begun to grow   200
Decides to marry, whom does he wed—
Not a girl who is finely-bred,
With fawn-like figure and fetching face,
Who knows how to carry herself with grace,

19. Crone: a withered old woman.

But a wicked witch or a female scrooge   205
Who gathered her dowry[20] by subterfuge!
That's what makes me sore and sorry,
Weak and weary and worn with worry,
That's what has me sad and sighing,
That's the cause of all my crying—   210
When I see a youth of vigour and verve,
Who's big and strong and has plenty of nerve,
Who's learnt the things that a man should know,
And is not averse to having a go,
Or an eager, frisky, frolicsome boy   215
Whose cheek is innocent and coy,
Badgered, bought, and bound for bed
With a ga-ga[21] old gipsy[22] gone in the head,
Or a she-desperado, defamed and defiled,
A villainous witch who would frighten a child,   220
A bilious bitch who's too fond of the bottle,
A hen-pecking hag you'd be aching to throttle.
My God! There's a goat with a middle-aged spread,
With one gammy leg and a golliwog's[23] head
Who has married today and is mated by now,   225
While a virgin like me goes untouched by the plough!
How is it my beauty no passion awakes?

20. Dowry: the money, property, and capital a wife brings to an arranged marriage.

21. Ga-ga: doting or senile person.

22. Gypsy: a member of a wandering race; also a contemptuous term for a woman with the implication of her being cunning, deceitful, and fickle.

23. Golliwog: an invented name for a black-faced, fuzzy-haired, and grotesquely dressed doll.

Don't tell me I haven't whatever it takes!
My mouth is sweet and my teeth are flashing,
My face is never in need of washing,   230
My eyes are green and my hair's undyed
With waves as big as the ocean's tide.
And that's not a half, nor a tenth, of my treasure:
I'm built with an eye to the maximum pleasure.
From throat to breast to little finger   235
I've plenty to make a fellow linger;
My waist is slim and my back's unbowed,
With the best of fittings I'm well-endowed;
A look at my legs would provide a thrill,
And what's between them is better still.   240
I'm not silly or stupid or snobbish or snooty—
I've bags of breeding and brains and beauty;
I'm not a slattern[24] who has no pride
Or a scamp that's never satisfied;
Or a lazy laggard lacking in life   245
But a female fit for a prince's wife.
If I were the same as the rest of the mob
And were known by all as a senseless slob
And hadn't the wit to do my bit—
Well then, I wouldn't complain of it;   250
But I'm always present to show my face
At any funeral that takes place,
At match or race or dance or fête,[25]

24. Slattern: a woman or girl who is untidy and slovenly in person and habits; also a slut.

25. Fête: a large-scale festival, entertainment, or fair.

Wherever the people congregate,
I'm always the one to stick out a mile,   255
Dressed as I am in the best of style.
My hair is powdered to a T,
My cap is starched impeccably,
My bright-hued hood has ribboned puffs,
My speckled gown has plenty ruffs,[26]   260
I never forget my rich-red cape
For its facings stress my alluring shape,
And my apron that's painted with forest scenes
Would draw the envy of royal queens.
High-heeled shoes I always wear,   265
The trimmest, most expensive pair,
Brooches and bracelets and gloves of silk,
And lace that flows like a flood of milk.
Don't think, by the way, I'm a shy, young tot
Or a timorous, trembling touch-me-not,   270
Don't think I wouldn't say 'boo' to a goose[27]—
You can take it from me I'm no recluse.
Why should I run away and hide?
My face is my fortune, my figure my pride.
You can bet your life that I'm on parade   275
At every hurling-match that's played,
At parties, meetings, races, sports,
And I've even attended the criminal courts;
At Mass each week, at the market fair,

___

26. Ruff: a fringe of real or artificial material (e.g., fur or feathers) used as a
trim along the edge of the hood or neckline of a garment.

27. Boo to a goose: to open one's mouth, to speak.

Wherever a man is in sight, I'm there! 280
But after all that, my patience is ending,
They've broken my heart—no more pretending—
Whatever I did was never enough
The answer was always a rebuff.
I had my fortune told by all 285
With cups and cards and crystal ball,
And there wasn't a tale you could read or tell
Concerning the moon's romantic spell
During Easter and Christmas and New Year's Day
For which I didn't at some time pray. 290
Each night beneath my pillow I'd put
A stocking filled with the freshest fruit:
Three times I fasted without a meal,
And it wasn't because of religious zeal;
In the river's flow I washed my clothes 295
Hoping to make some man propose;
Often I went and swept the byre[28]
And my nails and hair I threw in the fire;
I placed a flail against the grate
And a spade by my bed to bring a mate; 300
Between two graves my stick I buried
And left my yarn where the lime is quarried;
Out on the road some flax I spread,
In the straw I stuck a cabbage-head;
All these I tried—trick upon trick— 305
And I prayed to Satan and all his clique,
You'd think by now I'd have some success,

---

28. Byre: a cow-shed or farmhouse.

But no—I'm still at the same address,
And what's worse—I haven't that youthful vigour
And soon I'll be losing my girlish figure;   310
The years won't wait, and I'm afraid
I'll die a miserable old maid.
Whatever else may be my lot
I'd suffer—anything but that;
Don't turn me loose at the end of my days   315
Like a gibbering goat with vacant gaze
Who, having no family or friend,
On cast-out leavings must depend.
By all the powers that live and rule,
But I must be the biggest fool   320
To remain unwed when feather-heads[29]
Are buckled each night in their double-beds.[30]
Beside her husband Sal[31] snores lightly,
Muirinn's[32] man can mate her nightly,
Fay and her fellow cuddle and kiss   325
And I am teased with what I miss.
Look at Cam[33] and her family growing
And Wendy's[34] womb is overflowing
So many around me are on the box
The people must think that I've the pox.   330

29. Feather-head: a silly, empty-headed, absent-minded person.
30. Double-bed: "full-sized" bed.
31. Sal: female personal name.
32. Muirinn (Muireann): female personal name.
33. Cam: female personal name.
34. Wendy: female personal name.

But I've been patient much too long—
I know a cure that can't go wrong,
A drink of herbs decayed I'll make
And this time there'll be no mistake,
I'll find a boy and with riddles quiz him   335
And raise his passion by hypnotism.
I've seen the others play that game
And now it's time I tried the same:
Many marriages begin
With spells from herbs and apple-skin,   340
A mandrake's root I'll find and use
And none will then my charms refuse;
I'll bite the stalk of a special grape
That's said to provoke a man to rape,
Or I'll sew old leaves beneath my dress,   345
And I've other ruses you'd never guess.
You were all surprised when a certain shrew
Was recently married (you know who),
Well, afterwards I heard her say
How it was done: All Souls' Day[35]   350
She feasted off a withered spider
That has soaked six weeks in cider!
I've waited like this till I'm sick and sore
So damned if I'm waiting any more,
And if you and your court can't help me now   355
I'll get me a man—and I don't care how!"

---

35. All Souls' Day: the commemoration of all the faithful departed is usually
celebrated annually by the Catholic Church on November 2.

The Midnight Court/Cúirt an Mheán Oíche

The second part, in which the poet hears a spirited and somewhat salty speech on behalf of the defence.

Then up there sprung, as if he'd been stung,
A wizened old josser,[36] and down he flung
His cap in rage, and danced on it,
Till people thought he'd thrown a fit;   360
And though not officially called to reply
He just looked at the girl, and then let fly:
"May doubts and dangers beat you flat
You jadey[37] lump of a beggar's brat!
It's no surprise that the sun won't shine,   365
That Ireland's fortunes still decline,
That all our rights are swept away,
That our cattle die and our crops decay
When you and your kind go unrebuked—
No wonder our goose is almost cooked!   370
Isn't it known to the biggest gom[38]
The breed that you're descended from,
And for all your boasting and high-class talk
They never did more than beg and hawk.[39]
Your father we can still recall   375
(And well we might, for he robbed us all!)

36. Josser: a simpleton or ordinary person.

37. Jadey: from jade, a term of reprobation applied to a woman. Also used playfully, as are *hussy* or *minx*. Jade also serves as a contemptuous name for an inferior breed of horse (a carthorse versus a riding horse).

38. Gom: a fool, a dimwitted person.

39. Hawk: to carry items from place to place and offer them for sale, often unlicensed.

A hulking brute of an ignoramus,
If we'd put him away there'd be none to blame us;
Not a stitch on his back or his hairy chest,
A disgrace to the race—the way he dressed.   380
D'ya know?—If I were to ask for bids
For himself and his wife and his tribe of kids,
And sell the lot with their rags and bags—
What I'd get wouldn't buy me a packet of fags![40]
Yet you have the cheek to stand there and prattle   385
Who never owned even a head of cattle,
Dressed to kill in the best of clothes
And a handkerchief held to protect your nose!
Others might judge you by what they see
But don't come trying your cod[41] on me;   390
I know what you wear and, upon me oath,
Your shanks[42] never rustled a petticoat
And in storms when your dress is blown high and wide
The world can gaze at your bare backside!
You talk of your figure, but isn't it grand   395
How stays can be faked with a canvas band!
Your brooches and jewels may dazzle and glow
But under your gloves your hands are a show;
And explain to the Court how much of a treat
It would be to have something to drink when you eat,   400
To go with the dry, unsalted spud
That the pigs leave buried in the mud.

40. Fags: cigarettes.
41. Cod: deception or lies.
42. Shank: the part of one's leg extending from the knee to the ankle.

19

And wouldn't your face be fine and red
If I divulged where you make your bed?
Not even a sheet beneath your bones   405
Or a bundle of straw to cover the stones
But a dirty old mat, ragged with filth,
And that's what serves for mattress and quilt
On the floor of a hut that hasn't a bench,
Where the mud is thick, and the ghastly stench   410
Of the cats and dogs and hens and cocks
Is enough to overcome an ox,
And so bad is the roof and the broken walls
That the weather can pay you constant calls.
Begob[43] but isn't she cool as a breeze,   415
In the best of gowns, and, if you please,
As harmless as Little Red Riding Hood,
But she didn't get them for being good.
Come on, you might as well admit
All that you had to exchange for it,   420
For you weren't elected a Fashion Queen,
And it's not so long since you hadn't a bean;
Or perhaps you'd prefer us to make a guess
As to how you came by your flashy dress,
And goodness knows what you had to lose   425
To achieve the price of those splendid shoes.
Aeval, listen to my report
And you'll throw that hussy out of court;
You'll pity the husbands of all these bitches
When I reveal who wears the breeches.   430

---

43. Begob (by God): an Anglo-Irish exclamation.

I was told by a pal—lives up the street—
As nice a lad as you'd ever meet,
A quiet, sober, decent man—
Until he married some harridan.[44]
It galls[45] me to see her on parade: 435
Such airs and graces as are displayed,
The way she boasts of her cows and crops
And opens accounts in the classiest shops.
I met her yesterday, face to face,
With her two fat breasts all over the place,   440
Swaying her hips like a ship in a storm
And generally running true to form;
Were it not for the fact that I'm discreet
And rather reluctant to repeat
The things I'm told, I could raise your hair   445
By recounting the times she's been stretched out bare,
On the flat of her back upon the ground
And the customers rushing from miles around,
From youth to grandad, all can speak
Of her adaptable technique—   450
In Ibrickane[46] with big and small,
In Teermaclane[47] with one and all,

44. Harridan: a haggard, decayed old woman, usually a term of vituperation.
45. Gall: annoy, irritate.
46. *Íbh Breacáin* (anglicized as Ibrickane): a coastal barony in west Clare, incorporating the parishes of Kilfarboy (Miltown Malbay) and Kilmurry Ibrickane. Merriman's family originated from this area.
47. *Tír Mhic Calláin/Tíortha Mhic Cuileáin* (anglicized as Teermaclane): a small hamlet and townland in the parish of Killone, barony of Islands, on the main Ennis to Kildysert road.

In Kilbrickane[48] with thick and thin,
In Clare,[49] in Ennis,[50] and in Quin,[51]
In Cratloe[52] and Tradree[53] where they're tough   455
She never seemed to have enough!
But I'd still have allowed her a second chance
And blamed it on youthful extravagance
Were it not that I saw with my own two eyes
On the roadway—naked to the skies—   460
Herself and a lout from the Durrus[54] bogs
Going hammer and tongs[55] like a couple of dogs.
To think of it now nearly makes me ill
For I'd never have thought it possible
For her to oblige that enormous queue   465
And not have a child till she wanted to.
But even so she cut it fine

48. *Cill Bhreacáin* (anglicized as Kilbreckane): a townland in the parish of Doora, barony of Bunratty Upper, on the main Quin-Ennis road. Merriman would have passed through it on his way from Feakle to Ennis town.

49. *An Clár* (anglicized as County Clare): an Irish county in the province of Munster.

50. *Inis* (anglicized as Ennis): County Clare's principal town.

51. *Cuinche* (anglicized as Quin): refers to a village, townland, and parish in the barony of Bunratty Upper in County Clare.

52. *Creatlach* (anglicized as Cratloe): a village and townland in the parish of Kilfintinan, barony of Bunratty Lower, on the road from Feakle to Limerick city.

53. *Tradraí* (anglicized as Tradraighe): part of the ancient territorial divisions of Thomond, it stretched from Bunratty on the river O'Garney in the east, to the estuary of the river Fergus in the west of County Clare.

54. *Dúire* (anglicized as Doorus): a townland in the parish of Feakle overlooking Lough Graney near where Merriman lived.

55. Going hammer and tongs: with great effort and energy.

And wasted precious little time,
For counting from the very date
That she renounced her single state   470
Until she bore a squalling brat
Was just nine months—and barely that.
Let every unmarried man take heed
And avoid being hooked by one of her breed,
Or he'll spend his life being bullied and bossed,   475
You can take it from me—for I know to my cost.
I remember when I was a bachelor
And I wonder now what I married for;
I had health and wealth and a reputation,
My name was a golden recommendation,   480
Treated by the Law with unction,
Asked to every high-class function,
People listened when I spoke
And laughed whenever I cracked a joke.
What more could I want? I thought I knew: 485
So I married—and landed in a stew.
I claimed at the time I did well to win her—
Plenty of eating and drinking in her,
Hair that was curled and soft to touch,
A look in her eye that promised much,   490
A laugh that was laced with implication,
A figure that offered an invitation—
All I craved was to be wed
And then to get her into bed;
But the bigger they are the harder they fall,   495
And Fate has fixed me for good and all;
My prayers were answered—to be sure—
But I got much more than I bargained for.

I saw that all was rightly done:
The clergy blessed our union,   500
I threw a party I'll never forget
And didn't leave a single debt;
And—fair is fair—there's none can say
That anyone was turned away.
The priest, who received a handsome fee,   505
Was as pleased as Punch[56]—and why wouldn't he be?
The guzzling crowds around the table
Sounded like the Tower of Babel;
And the drink it took to stock the bar
Was enough to float a man-o'-war!   510
A pity indeed that I wasn't drowned
At birth, or at least before I found
The urge to marry that old crock
And make myself a laughing-stock.
Not that I wasn't tipped the wink   515
About the name she had for drink
And how she'd sleep with anyone—
Married or single, father or son.
For long I wouldn't believe a word
And laughed at everything I heard   520
Till people wondered what I'd do
When I'd find their tales were true.
How right they were—but none can be
As blind as him who will not see.

---

56. As pleased as Punch: extremely pleased, proud; Mr. Punch is a hook-nosed, humpbacked character from the British children's Punch and Judy show.

I said it was gossip that couldn't be proved—   525
Until her corset was removed,
And I saw that they hadn't exaggerated—
For, contrary to orthodoxy,
Someone had made me a father by proxy!
But that wasn't all that happened to me—   530
I awoke next day with a family!
A baby screaming, women prating,
My wife in bed recuperating,
Water on the hob[57] to heat,
A bottle fitted with a teat,   535
Everyone at action-stations
And the midwife directing operations.
Around the fire neighbours gathered
Nodding and winking as they blathered,
And one was saying as she smiled: 540
'The blessings of God be on the child!
Though he's come a wee bit premature
You can see the da[58] in him for sure;
Look at his shape: there isn't a bit
That isn't the old man's living spit,   545
And there's legs for you, and arms and wrists,
Did you ever see such a pair of fists?'
They said that by natural statistics
The child was blessed with my characteristics:

57. Hob: the back of the chimney or grate on which things were placed to heat
or remain warm.
58. Da: a short form of Daddy.

The nose and brow aristocratic,   550
Chin determined and emphatic,
Even our laughter was compared—
Everything I had, he shared.
Meanwhile I hadn't seen his lordship—
Exposing him would be too much hardship,   555
And claiming that draughts would kill the mite
They kept him hidden from my sight.
I need hardly tell you that by this stage
They had me in a proper rage—
I cursed and damned them well and truly   560
Threatening to become unruly
Until they gave the child to me
With, 'Mind, he bruises easily!
A fall his mother had, I'd say,
Has brought him on before his day;   565
Don't squeeze him hard, and keep him steady,
His life is short enough already,
'Tis barely possible with care
He'll last until the priest is here.'
He was bundled in blankets as protection,   570
And I removed them for better inspection;
I declare to God! But there on my knees
Was a bloody pocket-Hercules,
Shoulders big and wide and square-cut,
Already he needed a man-sized haircut!   575
His ears were like sails, and his nails were long,
And his biceps bulging like King Kong!
His nose was thick and his eyes were cocky,
His legs were made for a champion jockey;
Matchless in mind and muscle and middle,   580

As tough as they come and as fit as a fiddle!
Your Worship, there's my tale in brief
And it's up to you to prescribe relief,
We need your help and firm decision
To save us from our wives' derision.   585
Revise the law of married couples
And grant the single man his scruples;
Don't heed the fall in the population
Or think we're a disappearing nation,
You'd see how quickly things improved   590
If some of the obstacles were removed.
What need is there for bridal veils
And taxis and organs and toppers and tails?
What good is all the fuss and racket?
Sure in drink alone you'd save a packet;   595
Besides, there's holy precedent
For births that aren't exactly meant
And nothing living can exceed
The top-class quality of that breed.
I've often seen them: big as horses,   600
Mighty limbs and massive torsos;
Irrespective of who bears them
Plague or sickness never scares them
For they're stronger and more fit
Than many that are legitimate.   605
To prove to you all that I'm far from wrong
I brought my specimen along:
He's tough and tawny and full of fight,
Has Your Worship ever seen such a sight?
Now doesn't he delight your eyes?   610
He's still a child, but what a size!

27

Built, as is clear, to a vast proportion
Without a blemish or distortion—
He isn't a weakling, pale and pawky,[59]
Or thin as a stalk, or lank and gawky;[60]   615
He isn't a softy, dopey and dumb,
But a brute you could use in a rugby scrum!
'Tis easy to tell that he wasn't bred
From a routine go in a marriage-bed
By any sleepy, tired old slob   620
Who hadn't the tools for such a job,
But sprung from a man who knew his stuff
And a woman who couldn't get enough!
He gives us proof we can't refute
By his every perfect attribute   625
That none can beat the illegal sire
Who's too good a marksman to hold his fire.
And so, Your Worship, keep no more
A law that myriads deplore,
Remove unreal impediments   630
From tinkers, tramps, and titled gents;
Let the proletariat
Mate with the aristocrat,
Proclaim the news throughout the land
That love is free and no longer banned,   635
And soon you'll see a warrior race
Springing up all over the place,
With every man and son and grandson

59. Pawky: having a sardonic sense of humor.
60. Gawky: awkward or ungainly.

As powerful and strong as Samson;[61]
The skies will smile; fish will abound,   640
Flowers and trees will smother the ground;
And the people will fulfil their function,
Singing your praises at every junction."

*The third part, in which the poet hears further derogatory charges against
the male sex in general and the previous speaker in particular.*

The girl, by now, had heard enough
And up she started in a huff,   645
She read your man the Riot Act,[62]
Paused for a breath, and then attacked:
"Lucky," says she, "that I've a care
For the fact that you're old and a little queer,
And that Her Worship might object   650
Or soon I'd teach you some respect.
I'd quickly put you out of action
And beat you down to a vulgar fraction[63]
Till, with a mighty final blow,
I'd send you on your way below.   655
It's certain no one takes as true
The stories of the likes of you,

61. Samson: a Biblical character noted for his strength.

62. The Riot Act, repealed in 1973, declared that if twelve or more persons
assembled and refused to disperse within an hour of the Act being read aloud to
them, they were deemed felons before the law.

63. A vulgar fraction, also referred to as a "common fraction," is a rational
number written as one integer divided by a non-zero integer.

But still I'll tell how you behaved
Towards the girl *you* say you saved:—
Reduced to begging from door to door   660
All she had were the rags she wore,
Exposed to every kind of weather
She'd all but reached the end of her tether—
Day after day, walking the street
With hardly a drink or a bite to eat.   665
And then this chancer happened by,
Fooled her up to the ball of her eye,
Promised her, if she'd be his wife,
Breakfast in bed for the rest of her life,
A separate banking account of her own,   670
A butler, a car, and a telephone,
And every month a brand-new gown,
With a country seat[64] and a flat[65] in town!
There wasn't a thought in anyone's mind
That it could have been love of the dimmest kind   675
Would make her consent as long as she'd live
Had she any better alternative.
Fat chance there was of a night's high jinks
With such a fossilised old sphinx;
What passion could a girl entice   680
From thighs as stiff and as cold as ice,
A hulk that a furnace couldn't heat,
A bag of bones, devoid of meat?
The saints themselves wouldn't expect

64. Seat: the residence of a country gentleman or nobleman.
65. Flat: an apartment.

A wife to stand for such neglect   685
From a hog of a husband whom nothing would stir
To see was she feather, fin, or fur;
Who, lure as she might, would never mate her
But lay like a human refrigerator.
Not that she set him too great a task   690
(Once per night wasn't much to ask!)
And don't imagine her modesty
Would scare a fellow from making free,
A lady she was from stem to stern—
But where's the wick that, when lit, won't burn?   695
She'd work all night—you can bet on that—
And at dawn she'd still give him tit for tat.[66]
She'd grant his pleasure whatever it be,
Her eyes aglaze with ecstasy,
She'd not ignore his eager questions   700
Or snap at him for his suggestions—
Down beside him she'd recline
Wound around him like a vine,
And trying to coax a flame to light
She'd kiss his lips and squeeze him tight.   705
His fancy she often attempted to tease
By rubbing against him from waist to knees;
She did her best to make him play
But there wasn't a move from that lump of clay,
He remained indifferent to all her tricks,   710
To kisses, caresses, scratches, and kicks.

---

66. Tit for tat: one blow in return for another; an equivalent given in return
(usually in the way of injury, rarely of benefit); retaliation.

I blush to reveal that he left her languish,
Gripping the bed-post, sobbing in anguish,
Bewailing the shame of a spotless sheet,
With frozen limbs and chattering teeth,   715
And she cried till dawn without cessation,
Tossing and turning in humiliation.
What neck he has, acting the critic,
That leprous, parlous paralytic;
His wife may have fooled him—but didn't he wrong her?   720
And—truly now—which of us would have been stronger?
What bear or badger, buck or beagle,
Leaping stag or wheeling eagle
Would gasp with thirst a single hour
And let the sweetest drink go sour?   725
I have the gravest doubt indeed
Whether a beast of any breed
Would look for food where nothing grows
And shun the meal beneath his nose.
Let's hear, you dolt, your fine defence   730
And see if it makes any sense
Was there anything missing that you can tell?
If not, then weren't you doing well?
Is a house devalued the slightest bit
If twenty million inspected it?   735
Don't be afraid, you poor old crock,
You wouldn't get in if you should knock.
Have you so large an appetite
That others shouldn't take a bite?
Don't fool yourself: it's plain to see   740
You couldn't exhaust a female flea!
Put your illusions well aside

Unless you want to be certified,
And don't be making such a fuss
Because the woman was generous—   745
She could handle a dozen a day, or more,
And toss you off as an encore!
Such jealousy would be no fault
In someone who was worth his salt,
A lusty lover, a proved romancer,   750
A fellow who wouldn't take 'no' for an answer,
Who'd not be stopped by etiquette,
Whose thrust would be sharp as a bayonet;
But there's more to fear from the prick of a thorn
Than from this old cow with a crumpled horn!   755
Another thing I'd like to mention
That's beyond my comprehension—
Whatever made the Church create
A clergy that is celibate?
The lack of men is a cruel curse   760
Just now when things were never worse;
I'd give my eyes to have a lover
The ripest, though, are under cover.
It's such a bitter pill to swallow
For one like me, who hasn't a fellow,   765
To see them big and strong of stature,
Full of charm and bright good-nature,
Each one seems a fresh young stripling,
Hard of bone and muscles rippling,
Backs as straight as a sergeant-major's,   770
And desires as keen as razors.
They live in the lap of luxury,
And, what's more, it's all tax-free;

Well-dressed, well-treated, and well-fed,
With warming-pans to heat their bed.   775
Man for man they'd beat the best,
And they're human like the rest.
I'd skip the ones who don't pass muster,
Raddled ancients who lack lustre,
But I'd soon shake up the one   780
Who snores while work is left undone!
Perhaps you'd find that quite a share
Would play the part, and those I'd spare,
For, after all, it wouldn't do
To damn the many for the few,   785
A sturdy ship should not be sunk
Because one sailor has no spunk!
We know that some are tough old terrors
Who would never mend their errors,
Frozen fogeys[67] who believe   790
God blundered when he fashioned Eve;
But others secretly admit
They think her nature's choicest bit!
There's many a house that didn't begin
To prosper and smile till the priest dropped in,   795
And many a woman could toss her head
And boast of the time he blessed her bed;
Throughout the land there's ample proof
The Church is anything but aloof,

---

67. Fogey: a man advanced in life often with antiquated notions and considered to be behind the times.

34

And many a man doesn't know that he   800
Has a son with a clerical pedigree.
But it's a shame the strength and time
They waste on women past their prime,
While others miss the best in life
Because a priest can't take a wife;   805
Just think of the massive population
This rule has cost the Irish nation!
It's for Your Honour to decide
What's mainly needed: priest or bride.
It seems to me a priest should know   810
Life's ups and downs; is that not so?
Tell us, that we may understand,
What was the Holy Book's command?
When was it the Creator said
That bodily appetites mustn't be fed?   815
Lust, said Paul,[68] and not a wife
Was something man should shun for life,
For indeed he advocated
Men and women should be mated.
Ah, but who am I to jaw[69]—   820
You're the one who knows the law;
That's what got you your degrees,
For you can recollect with ease
Every sentence, every word
Of all the sayings of the Lord;   825

68. St. Paul the Apostle.
69. Jaw: to talk.

They should be in our favour, for
The Lord Himself was no bachelor.
Before Your Honour now I plead,
O prophetess of royal seed,
O shining glory of the race,   830
A word from you would solve our case.
Weigh up the merits on our side,
Consider each potential bride,
And see how quickly they increase,
Multiplying like the geese;   835
The most repulsive ones you'd find—
The hags, the bags, the semi-blind,
If they but had the right injection
Overnight they'd change complexion,
They would lose their present color   840
And parade in Technicolor!
But is it any use at all
To beat our heads against a wall—
I see no chance of having fun
With men outnumbered three to one.   845
And since so few can fill the bill,
Since times are bad and prospects nil,
With too much talk from old rapscallions[70]
Who'd be better off as stallions,
And since girls who get the chance   850
Must go for anything in pants,
Give me a man and hold him down
And then just watch me go to town!"

70. Rapscallion: a rascal, rogue, vagabond, scamp.

The fourth part, in which the poet hears the verdict—and is suitably impressed.

Aeval arose, all charm and grace,
And sunshine seemed to fill the place.   855
Her features had the glow of youth,
Her voice was strong—the voice of truth.
The bailiff rapped to stop the talk
And glared and glowered like a hawk;
The chatter slowly died, until   860
She spoke, and then the Court was still:—
"My girl," she said, "I must declare
Your treatment has been far from fair.
I cannot but be shocked to know
Our women's plight has sunk so low,   865
Unwanted, haggard, tired, sore,
Turned away from every door;
And that the country's on its ear
Exploited by each racketeer.
So grab each male who's still unmarried   870
At twenty-one, and have him carried
And tied unto the nearest tree,
And make quite sure he can't break free;
Strip him of his coat and shirt
And flay him till he's really hurt.   875
Adults who never stood at stud,
Whose weapon was a perfect dud,
Who never even tried to use it,
Never bothered to amuse it,
Never got their powder hot,   880
Just sat upon their balls and shot,
Their penance can be settled by

The girls whom they left high and dry.
Expose them to a roaring fire,
Use any methods you desire,   885
You'll pick some tough ones, I expect,
But go ahead, I'll not object;
Wreak vengeance on such useless men—
Sudden death's too good for them.
We hardly need to pay attention.   890
To those who draw the old-age pension,[71]
They're too weak to show the flag
Which hardly has the strength to wag;
But from the young take no evasion,
Make them rise to the occasion.   895
Plenty men fight poverty
And still support a family,
Their strength and spirit never wilt,
They back their wives up to the hilt,
They work and play and love and breed;   900
And that's the sort of men we need.
I've heard a rumour go the rounds—
Though not upon the best of grounds,
So keep it quiet, do not spread it—
No authority has said it   905
But the Church may soon allow
The priests to take the marriage-vow;
And then they'll live life to the full
Encouraged by a Papal Bull.[72]

71. Old-age pension: a form of social security available at the age of sixty-five.
72. Papal Bull: a letter, edict, or mandate from the Catholic Pope.

They have the best material   910
For such pursuits venereal,
And indeed the merest prick
Is all they need to do the trick.
I think I've mentioned every male
That's known unto the social scale,   915
Don't break the rule for anyone,
For hangman, half-caste, or Right Hon.,[73]
But root them out and drive them forth
Out of the country or up North.
Well now, I must be on my way,   920
I've much to do and can't delay,
I'm sure that you will understand
My tour of duty's firmly planned.
But I'll return, and then God save
The worthless and unmarried knave,   925
And those whose thoughts are mean and low,
Who tell their pals which girls will 'go,'
Who boast of every victory
As if it merits a V.C.;[74]
They think there's no one else on earth   930
Who's got inside a woman's skirt.
And not that love provokes their heat
And drives them to be indiscreet,
Not from the artist's pride they crow
But from sheer braggadocio.[75]   935

73. Right Hon.: Right Honorable, an honorific prefix.
74. V.C.: Victoria Cross, a military decoration awarded for valor.
75. Braggadocio: empty boasts.

Nor are they honest Rabelais's[76]
But scamps[77] who swim in false self-praise,
Who, though they're voluble of tongue,
Their withers[78] often are unwrung;
They talk enough, but how they'd flinch   940
If they but saw a bare square-inch!
And now I'll have to leave you here
For I am overdue elsewhere,
But have no doubt I'll make things hum
For bachelors, when next I come."   945
I'd listened to Her Worship speak,
And when she stopped I felt quite weak,
My blood grew cold, then hot and fizzy,
And my head was sick and dizzy;
Walls and roof went in and out   950
While what she'd said rang round about.
The ugly bailiff rose in sight
And grabbed at me up before the Bench.[79]
The girl who'd made the first protest
Clapped hands, and screamed, and beat her chest;   955
"You fraud," she shouts, as up she springs,
"I've waited long to clip your wings,
You thought you left me on the shelf,
But now I have you to myself,

76. Rabelais: François Rabelais (circa 1494 to 9 April 1553), a major French Renaissance writer, humanist, and avant-garde writer of fantasy and satire. Associated with grotesquery, dirty jokes, and bawdy songs.
77. Scamp: a rascal, a mild term of reproof.
78. Withers: the highest part of a horse's back, between the shoulder-blades.
79. Bench: the seat where judges sit in court; the seat of justice.

And once your head is in my noose   960
You can pickle your excuse.
I know your talent may be small
But did you try it once at all?
Inspect him, girls, at your ease:
He has the right accessories;   965
Examine what he has to show
From the top of his head to his little toe;
Although you'll find some slight misfits
He has a male's prerequisites.
His colour's not what one'd expect   970
And his back is bowed—but I'd not object
To taking a fellow who has a hump—
It's not in his back he keeps his trump!
And often a gaffer with gammy pins[80]
Becomes the father of quads[81] or quins.[82]   975
There's some dark mystery unknown
That's made this blackguard[83] live alone,
For lords salute him when they pass
And he has friends in every class;
At high-tone functions he's a guest,   980
And when he's there they serve the best;
He's had enough of selfish pleasure,
Now at last we have his measure.
His name is one we must applaud:

80. Pins: colloquial term for legs.

81. Quads, quadruplets: a set of four children born at the same birth.

82. Quins, quintet: a set of five children born at the same birth.

83. Blackguard: vagabond. The word has an implication of criminality or anti-social behavior.

'Merriman,' but it's a fraud;   985
He must have been baptised in haste—
For though he's old he still is chaste.
I'll teach the likes of him a lesson
And I'll suffer no digression;
His face provides a full admission: 990
Thirty years without coition!
Now, my hearties, be prepared,
No endeavour must be spared;
Recall the times that we were spurned,
But here, at last, the worm has turned.   995
All hands now! Help! Hold down the pup!
Run, Una! Rope him! Tie him up!
Push, Anne! You can do better surely!
Mary, tie his hands securely!
Sheila, Sal, don't stand and stare   1000
Hurry now, and do your share,
You heard his punishment announced
So see he's well and truly trounced,
Lay into him each time you hit,
His bottom's broad enough for it;   1005
Just keep on striking where he bends,
You'll soon reduce his fat, my friends,
Don't weaken, don't be faint of heart,
You're not to miss a single part.
Beat hard so that his screams and cries   1010
Will freeze the other nancy-boys.
No better day than this could be,
It should go down in history,
So write it out, and don't forget
We may be all quite famous yet—"   1015

She took her pen; I gave a moan;
Her threats had chilled me to the bone;
And as she scribbled in a book
And eyed me with a dreadful look,
I took a breath that was long and deep,   1020
And opened my eyes—I had been asleep.

Part Two

Cúirt an Mheán Oíche

A Wonder of Ireland

ALAN TITLEY

*W*hat is it about *Cúirt an Mheán Oíche/The Midnight Court* that summons us to listen to its call? Why does one poem from the west coast of Ireland still exercise the mind and imagination of translators, scholars, social historians, and the general public two hundred years after the poet's death? There is no other Irish poem that has been translated, wholly or in large part, into five different languages by some sixteen different translators commencing with a translation by Denis Woulfe less than twenty years after Merriman's death until the latest rollicking translation by Ciarán Carson published in 2006. Within the Irish tradition it would be easy to pluck out a gabble of poets whose work is more central and important than Merriman's: Dáibhí Ó Bruadair, Aogán Ó Rathaille, Eoghan Rua Ó Súilleabháin, and Séamas Dall Mac Cuarta. Nevertheless, *Cúirt an Mheán Oíche* is undoubtedly the most famous Irish poem of all.

A recent survey on glossy magazines concluded that the word "sex" on a front cover sells more copies. It might just be, therefore, that sex "sells" *Cúirt an Mheán Oíche*, so to speak. As you strip away, if I may use that phrase, the various layers, it becomes clear that it is about all those ancillary things too: clerical celibacy, marriage, old men, young women, and illegitimate children. This is the stuff of perennial debate—and what sells tabloids; it is *Stud, Cosmopolitan, Hello,* and *Nuts* without the twenty-first century gloss. It is also rolling, rambunctious, thumping, even thrusting, poetry, some of which comes across in the best translations. Added to this is a certain mystery about Merriman himself, whose name is the subject of dispute: is it Merriman, Merryman, Mac Giolla Meidhre, or McNamara? The fact that he appears in the poem invites speculation that he was born outside of marriage, or was a priest's son, or suffered some serious trauma that prompted the poem.[1] What is important about Merriman, as it is for any writer, is what was inside his head. And what was inside his head was much more exciting than the life he probably led. Literature is about words and expression and the way they are put together. Literature is largely about literary performance. And very often it is about what to do with words, despite ideas. One of *Cúirt an Mheán Oíche*'s great problems is that it became a battleground for ideas, social mores, Éamon de Valera's Ireland, the nature of Irish literature, the Enlightenment, demography, and more.

The poem opens in what seems a very conventional way. Lovers of common ballads will recognize the archetypal scene in these two random examples:

> As I went out on a May morning
> On a May morning quite early
> I met my love upon the way
> And, Lord but she was curly.

1. I will not discuss them here, except to say that I think Brian Ó Dalaigh's suggestion of Merriman being a form of "Marrinan" or "Marrannáin" seems to make sense, and that there is no evidence for his being an illegitimate child of a priest, a pauper, or a poet.

and again:

> As I went a-walking one morning in May
> To view the fine fields and the valley so gay
> I met with a young girl so sweet and so fair
> And the other was a soldier and a brave grenadier.

In Irish we have hundreds of them—all entirely unrealistic, of course. Scholars long thought it carried a deep social truth about Ireland. The notion that Merriman addresses a deep social problem—the problem of the falling population and the refusal of the mate to mate with his mate—was for many years proposed as the poem's central argument. This argument is easily refuted. Never in Ireland did the population grow as fast as when Merriman wrote. Indeed "[b]etween the middle of the eighteenth century and 1820 population grew at a rapid rate, averaging between 1.6 and 1.7 per cent annually" (Mokyr and Ó Grada 1984, 476). All the facts bear this out. Demographers show Ireland's population at less than four million when Merriman was writing. The 1821 census found about seven million people in Ireland, which reflected a population explosion of about 70 percent in less than two generations. I have never quite understood why people read this poem as a social document, at least as regards the facts of the situation. There are fascinating pieces about social practices (for example, Ó hAnluain 2000, 153–67) hidden in the corners of *Cúirt an Mheán Oíche,* but these were palpably not the reasons Merriman wrote his great poem.

Cúirt an Mheán Oíche is a story about a court. The first person up is a young woman who has not succeeded in ensnaring her man despite using every available trick. She tells of her talents, beauty, and glories. When she is finished, a man replies. His own story is part of the poem's high Chaplinesque broad humor—slapstick, farce, and mockery. But I think it best not to examine the logic of *Cúirt an Mheán Oíche,* either in social terms or in terms of character. The man's case ends with a passionate plea for free love—everybody should be allowed to propagate with whomsoever they desire, and bastards (a term used in several translations) are more likely to be healthy and strong because they were conceived in passion, rather than being the compliant offspring of an arranged union. Marriage, then, is seen as the enemy of great fertility, vigor, and life.

The young girl further argues that he was old and of little use in bed, which is, of course, a long-established theme in both folk and literary poetry. We have similar themes in countless Irish and Hiberno-English poems and ballads. In French this type of poetry is known as the *chanson de la malmariée,* and similar English ballads abound, such as "An Old Man Came Courting Me":

> There was an old man came over the sea
> Faith but I won't have him
> There was an old man come over the sea
> Came sniffling snuffling all around me
> With his long grey beard
> With his long grey beard
> A'shiverin' and shakin'

But her conclusion is simple enough, a conclusion with which the judge agrees. It does not matter whom women marry as long as men provide the respectability of marriage. Those who argue that Merriman had revolutionary ideas about love and life might equally argue that he was a most conventional thinker. The juicy part of the girl's oration is, however, her admission that what women really desire are priests. We must remember that priests in rural communities were the rock stars and celebrities of their day.[2] But at the end of the poem something strange happens. In a poem so artistically composed, so carefully choreographed, so craftily organized, we expect a resolution. Most commentators think that we are disappointed. The poem, in Frank O'Connor's words, "falls away" (1945, 10). In his 1945 introduction he writes: "After that, from the moment when the Queen gets up to deliver judgment, the poem falls away. Clearly this was intended to be the point at which Merriman would speak through her, and express his own convictions about life, but something went wrong" (10). Sean Ó Tuama rightly adds that it is because Merriman really had nothing new or momentous or world-shattering to say about life, marriage, or the problems of living (1995, 74). He might have added that there is very little new under the sun, it is all in the way you tell it. And Merriman told it with gusto, life, passion, fun, self-deprecation, humor, and a devil-may-care attitude. Aoibheall's (anglicized Aeval) judgment may be evil according to men, but no doubt it has a certain logic within the poem and may have resonance for misanthropic creatures everywhere. Basically what she says is that the women should beat seven kinds of crap out of men, using torture, flagellation, and skin-stripping. Indeed you could argue that it is supposed to be not only a poem about the twilight of eighteenth-century Ireland, but a poem designed to give succor to sadomasochists everywhere, that is, if you accept simple sociological or psychological explanations regarding the poem. But, of course,

---

2. Some people may recognize unintended references to Irish clerical history of the last ten years or so in the young girl's summation in which she appeals for an end to clerical celibacy. At this stage we begin to see the perennial fascination of Merriman's poem.

this is most certainly not what the poem is about at all. The end is even more anticlimactic. It appears for all intents and purposes to be an addendum, although it does bring the poem full circle.

To return to our initial question, what is all the fuss about? My own suspicion is that the poem is a work of art to which we—I do not exclude myself—can assign our own prejudices. I have already mentioned and disposed of those critics who saw it as social realism.[3] Beyond the social realists we have the biographical critics, those who see Merriman making a statement about himself, his birth, or his social status. They see the poem as some kind of catharsis, a confession, a code for his wounds and his life's incompletion. We need not, I think, look for a personal wound to get to the guts of Merriman. There were also those who wanted to use Merriman for their own cultural, social, or literary battles. The greatest of these was, without doubt, Frank O'Connor, whose take on the poem was certainly graphic. His translation, I believe, is among the best three we have, and in the introduction he suggests:

> Even with compulsory education, the English language, and pub-
> lic libraries you would be hard set to find a young Clareman of
> Merryman's class today who knew as much of Lawrence and Gide
> as he knew of Savage, Swift, Goldsmith and, most of all, Rousseau.
> How he managed it in an Irish-speaking community is a mys-
> tery. He was obviously a man of powerful objective intelligence;
> his obituary describes him as a "teacher of mathematics" which
> may explain something; and though his use of "Ego Vos" for the

---

3. To see it thus would be like saying that Dostoyevsky's novels showed a society in which people were intent on murdering little old ladies, or Jane Austen's England was a society in which dropping a handkerchief on the lawn during a picnic became a metaphysical truth.

marriage service suggests a Catholic upbringing, the religious background of *The Midnight Court* is Protestant, which may explain more. He certainly had intellectual independence. In *The Midnight Court* he imitated contemporary English verse, and it is clear that he had resolved to cut adrift entirely from traditional Gaelic forms. (O'Connor 1945, 5–6)

It may be that there is not one defensible sentence in that piece. O'Connor takes a large swipe at Éamon de Valera's Ireland, an Ireland that he felt had rejected him.[4] Another section from O'Connor's introduction is relevant as it raises the issue of clerical celibacy:

Then as the argument in favour of free love is developed, the girl bursts into a furious attack on clerical celibacy. This is where Merriman's audacity reaches its height, for, after all, he was writing in an Irish-speaking village in the eighteenth century things which even Yeats himself might have thought twice of writing in English-speaking Dublin of the twentieth, and yet he never once loses his bland and humane humour and is as full of pity for his well-fed canons and curates who have to conceal their indiscretions as he is for his young women. It is superb comedy, kept well in character; but then, once more we get the shifting of planes and the sudden intensity; the character of the woman drops away, and we are face to face with Bryan Merryman, the intellectual Protestant and disciple of Rousseau, with his appeal to scripture. (O'Connor 1945, 9)

There is here, of course, a confusion of realms, and a vital misunderstanding of Irish literature. In another place, in the introduction to

---

4. There is some irony in that it is reputed that De Valera knew *Cúirt an Mheán Oíche* by heart, a fact that gives the lie to De Valera's much-vaunted Puritanism.

Alan Titley

his great book of translations *Kings, Lords and Commons,* O'Connor argues that Merriman was "deeply influenced by the ideas of the Enlightenment and particularly by Burns" (1970, xiv). When it was pointed out that Robbie Burns lived after Merriman, O'Connor's answer in subsequent editions was "but the thing is impossible. He must derive from Burns" (xiv). O'Connor believed that the ideas put into the characters' mouths could not possibly exist in Irish-speaking Ireland. One of the early editors of the poem, Risteárd Ó Foghludha, makes the same point in a slightly different way. He says that "In the history of modern Gaelic literature two strikingly original figures stand out—Keating and Merriman—and the latter was the more original of the two" (Béaslaí 1912, 1). In other words, Merriman was different; he got his ideas from the great movements of European literature, he imitated English verse, he attempted to drag Ireland into the eighteenth century, even in 1780. Merriman was highly intelligent and probably widely read. And no less than any other open-minded Irish person of his time, he was aware of what was going on in the greater world. Living your life in Irish and writing in that language does not mean your brain does not go beyond Irish shores. There is nothing in *Cúirt an Mheán Oíche* that is new or original or surprising except in the way the poet uses the material. The meter had been used for long poems since the seventeenth century. The idea of a debate, an *agallamh beirte* is common in Irish poetry at least since the composition of *Fiannaíocht* or Fianna poetry. We have already shown that the question of the old man and the young woman, and the superior attributes of the child born "on the wrong side of the blanket" were common. The more we examine the poem, the more we see it as a work of its time, its place, and its reason of composition.

Scholar Liam P. Ó Murchú has shown convincingly that the poem was probably written for a court of poetry in Ennis, County

A Wonder of Ireland

Clare, in April 1780 (2005, 9). A court of poetry was simply an assembly of poets and people interested in poetry who gathered to discuss their work.[5] As the court served to discuss and assess poetry and had bailiffs, sheriffs, and judges, we see the ready comparison between a "court" of poetry, and *Cúirt an Mheán Oíche*. Merriman's poem may be no more than an elaborate play on the idea of a court of poetry. But the important point is that poems were read aloud for enjoyment, word-play, competition, and most important, for performance. Merriman, no more than any writer ever, tested himself against himself, but also tested himself against the assembly. We must imagine what it was like when Merriman rose to read his poem before the assembly.[6] Daniel Corkery describes such poetic courts/*cúirteanna éigse:* "Besides this reciting of verse and the discussions that followed, those gatherings enabled poets to borrow manuscripts and to examine such manuscripts. . . . They had no publishers, no laws of copyright, no press, no printers: it was, therefore, in such Courts that many a famous poem was heard for the first time" (2004, 103–4). We are fairly certain that the poem was first recited at such a gathering. Not only is it a poem, but it is also a play. We are often prisoners of the twentieth-century's conception of poetry as a thing of anguish and angst. In contrast, the highest accolade in the court was to be full of fun, and life, and energy. Poetry had to be *súgach,* that is to say "merry," even "drunk," as in drunk with life. Poets were asked to practice their art with *lúcháir,* with joy. They were asked to write their poems *i leabhraibh suairce,*

5. Such a court of poetry still exists in Cúil Aodha in West County Cork to the present day.

6. Daniel Corkery offers a wonderful picture of what a Court of Poetry might have been like in *The Hidden Ireland*. It is almost sloppily romantic, but why should we suppose it does not contain great truth? See Corkery (2004, 103–4).

in "books of gaiety," and an Irish "Court of Poetry" was a place of *greann agus cuideachta* (fun, wit, and company). These are the words that we meet again and again, words that denote geniality, cheerfulness, and levity. Poetry is the opposite of dullness. *Scuir den leamhas* (banish banality) may have been their motto. The subject matter of those poems could be anything. We have examples of poems about hares, horses, cows, the theft of a feather, and even a misshapen turnip. A very similar form of poetry, often practiced in the court of poetry, was the *barántas* (warrant). The *barántas* has examples whose subject matter is as noble as the theft of a cock, a quilt, a goose, a hat, a pig, or a piece of wood. This is craftsmanship and supreme wordcraft. Humor was the best way of entertaining the assembly, and word magic raised it to a higher art. Early descriptions of Merriman's poem all describe it as "humorous," "facetious," or "witty" or as a "burlesque." Only much later with our critical, psychologically superstitious, twentieth-century minds do we come to search for a "meaning" beyond what the text yields. Merriman was a bawdy writer—not smutty, sexy, dirty, or sly and definitely not erotic, impure, indecent, immodest, or salacious. He was just bawdy, Rabelaisian, ribald, and racy. And bawdiness is more an attribute of style, exhibitionism, and writing than anything else. Bawdiness was one of the traits of the courts of poetry, and bawdiness is more prevalent in the literature of Clare, Limerick, and North Kerry than in any other area.[7] Thomas F. O'Rahilly lists poets from the Clare area who had vulgar poems to their credit

7. A great folk singer like Con Greaney from Athea, County Limerick, could sing a song about "Nancy Hogan's Goose" without the slightest self-consciousness, and it is a song, incidentally, where a gander is arraigned in court for, as the words have it, "threading" the goose.

or discredit (1993, ix). Merriman was part of this, just as he was part of his time and his place.

So let us once again try to imagine what it was like in that court of poetry/*cúirt éigse* in Ennis or in Cuinche when Merriman recited his poem. We can be fairly sure also that a priest, or priests, attended the court, as was common practice. We can also be fairly certain that women attended the court, as we have evidence of women being elected to the highest office in such courts and participating in the literary haggling.

It is entirely possible that *Cúirt an Mheán Oíche* is one big elaborate and humorous commentary on the courts of poetry. The audience understood the inversion of the *aisling* form, the reluctant bachelor, the girl on the edge of the shelf, the horny clergy, *piseoga*, and superstitions. They understood them all because all of them were in the folk-mind already because they saw them all around them, but more than that, they understood them because he was talking about them! We can be sure that they laughed at themselves, as Merriman laughed at himself. He is, after all, a character in his own poem, and presents himself with self-deprecating fun. And we can be sure that he expected the audience to laugh at themselves, or at caricatures of themselves, as they do in every comedy ever written. The famous, or infamous, ending that both Frank O'Connor and Seán Ó Tuama saw as an anticlimax, is no such thing. In this ending, the women are allowed to strip and scourge the unmarried men of Ireland. But the audience—and we must always remember the audience—would instantly recognize it as a conventional ending, the most conventional ending in Irish poetry that parodied the English system of law. In *Barántas* or *Whereas* poems, the culprit who is hunted down is always subjected to the rigors of some law. These punishments always entail *"peannaidí pianghonta pionóis"* (painful poisonous punishments) even as far as death, because of satire, or lack of satisfaction in the theft of a head of cabbage, or the unlawful loan of a castrated ram.

Most modern commentators like to aver that it has something to do with the social situation in Clare, or women's liberation, or women's oppression, or the case of the long-suffering bachelors, or clerical celibacy, or the state of marriage, or the way things should be, or about Merriman himself, his birth, his habits, his background. The more I read the poem, and the more I read of eighteenth-century Irish-language literature, especially of the Clare, Limerick, and North Kerry region, the more I am convinced that the first people who heard it, laughed at it, and copied it were correct. It is a comic, burlesque poem. It is a play. It is a piece of invention using life and the imagination just as most writers have done since the beginning of time. We do not pretend that Synge had something profound to say about patricide when he wrote the *Playboy of the Western World,* or that Homer saw wandering on the sea as the supreme experience when he composed the *Odyssey.* That it is funny does not mean that we should not take it seriously. Humor is the compliment that intelligence pays to the serious, just as solemnity is the insult that dullness pays to intelligence. If we knew enough about them we would find that Merriman was not hugely different in mentality or in subject matter, or indeed, in the manner of his life, to many other poets of his time. What made him different was his wonderful mastery of language. He wrote an Irish that was both literary and colloquial. It is Irish in its full glow and strength and suppleness. It flows like the River Shannon, soars like an eagle, sparkles like the ocean, chuckles inwardly, and laughs out loud—but it never gets out of control. It is, and remains, one of the wonders of Ireland.

The Two Enlightenments of Brian Merriman's County Clare

MICHAEL GRIFFIN

*T*he intellectual background of Brian Merriman's *Cúirt an Mheán Oíche/The Midnight Court,* and the relative weightings of its ostensible cultural and intellectual provenances, are issues which have long exercised Irish literature's most accomplished scholars:

> Because of such ideas the poem has been looked on in the past as a work of the eighteenth-century Enlightenment, owning its inspiration to authors such as Rousseau, Voltaire and Swift. This view would scarcely be accepted nowadays. Indeed it has been pointed out that much of the thematic material in *The Midnight Court* is found already in that bawdy part of the courtly thirteenth-century *Roman de la Rose* which was added on to the original by Jean de Meung. . . . It is extremely doubtful, however, if Brian Merriman would have read any part of the *Roman de la Rose* in either French or English. How then did a teacher of mathematics in Feakle, County Clare in the year 1870 become familiar with the medieval court of love conventions? (Ó Tuama 1995, 64)

Sean Ó Tuama's essay, "Brian Merriman and His Court," composed originally in 1981, opens the question of the origins of Merriman's

59

Michael Griffin

great work; in so doing, he disavows the notion that the poem is in some way a product of the Enlightenment of Rousseau, Voltaire, and Swift and chooses instead to emphasize its place in the medieval European tradition of *Court of Love* poetry. Having tallied these two strands in favor of the latter tradition, he goes on to conclude that, whatever the poem's generic and intellectual influences, "the deeper feelings he is expressing throughout are the archaic feelings of his own traditional society" (Ó Tuama 1995, 76). A closer look at developments in County Clare suggests, however, that any one of those strands need not be emphasized at the expense of any other; indeed, to do so might be to neglect substantial elements of the poem's context and its achievement. As Declan Kiberd argues, "that Merriman managed to express the new Enlightenment ideas of 'freedom and social mobility' in 'that contemporary emergent world' is an awesome technical as well as intellectual achievement" (2000, 201). In other words, Merriman's sentiments regarding the threat faced by his community and his culture were filtered through an interweaving of Irish- and non-Irish-speaking enlightenments. Neil Buttimer opines that:

> this confirmation of the "Court's" textual interdependence, and, arising from it, the identification of a wider remit, may also encourage speculation on its indebtedness to other broadly based formative influences, particularly those of a more recent kind. The decade preceding its completion saw almost unprecedented levels of publishing on societal organization, internationally and with respect to Ireland, by philosophers, economists and the like. Descriptions of Clare itself, reminiscent of such writings, were made by authors also active in Gaelic composition, suggesting that others from the county, such as Merriman, might not have been immune from these trends. A short five years earlier, the outbreak of the American Revolution in 1775, ongoing until

60

Two Enlightenments of Merriman's County Clare

1782, would have involved widely publicized discussion of government, focusing on the need to end exclusiveness, for instance. North America, furthermore, would not have been unknown in the Irish-language community for its imagined climate of moral toleration. (2006, 345–46)

The intellectual and literary life of his native county was in a phase of acceleration just as Merriman was composing *Cúirt an Mheán Oíche,* as Louis Cullen has written (1996, 186–88). In Ennis, Clare's principal town, a quorum of talented poets writing in Irish was gathering to recite from, and exchange, manuscripts. Added to this, local print culture was taking off. Clare's first printing press arrived in Ennis in 1778, when John Busteed and George Trinder launched their *Clare Journal,* the first newspaper published in the county—the second paper, the *Ennis Chronicle,* would be launched in 1784. Though Dublin and Limerick newspapers and magazines such as *Pue's Occurrences, Faulkner's Dublin Journal,* and the *Limerick Journal* circulated widely in Ennis and through County Clare from the 1720s onward, local printing galvanized the rise of English in the county; thus, Irish came to be characterized as an oral or manuscript language at the same time that English became the printed language.

The *Clare Journal* sold at three halfpence, and was printed every Monday and Thursday. Newspaper circulations in Clare were in the range of three hundred to five hundred. Print culture, however, took no real cognizance of any Irish-speaking culture in the county. The *Clare Journal* was directed primarily at local well-to-do Protestants. Most of its materials were English-language reports of foreign news; the emphasis was Anglocentric, certainly, but there was a special concern with events in America. British packets were the primary source for London affairs, and leading news items were often reprints from the *London Gazette*. Between the 1770s and the 1790s, newspapers in Clare facilitated the development of a connection from the local to the national, and from the national to the international. Though the county's citizens were kept informed of revolutionary developments in America and France, the bias of the paper was certainly for the establishment.

The poetry published in the *Clare Journal* in Merriman's time usually traded in safer, upper-class sentiments. On 23 November 1778, for instance, the *Clare Journal* published "The Young Lady's Choice":

> Let the bold youth who aims to have me,
> know, I hate a fool, a clown, a sot, a beau:
> I loathe a sloven, I despise a cit,
> I scorn a coxcomb, and I fear a wit
> Let him be very rich and very kind,
> Charm'd with my virtues, to my follies blind
> Let him be gentle, brave, good humour'd, gay;
> Let him in smaller things with pride obey.
> Yet wise enough, in great ones to command,
> Produce me but the youth, and here's my hand.

As a poem of advice for the marriage market, this piece is lively enough; it would blush, however, in the company of *Cúirt an Mheán Oíche*. Comparing the poetry and the politics of the *Clare Journal* with those of poets like Merriman, we can see that there are two enlightenments under way in late-eighteenth-century Clare, a "polite," upper-class Angloglot enlightenment, and a more subversive enlightenment in the lower, Irish-speaking strata. Print was a medium through which local public spheres could absorb the political and poetical discourses of the world at large; and yet, there was another local public sphere, communicating and writing in Irish and transmitting through manuscript, of which Brian Merriman was almost certainly a part. These enlightenments, and their public spheres, were not without interesting interactions; nonetheless, they emitted rather different political and poetic tones.

The *Clare Journal* was never too adventurous when it came to politics. In the political sphere, indeed, the local papers would seek to act as a calming agent through the politically turbulent 1790s, as the activities of the radical United Irishmen, influenced by revolutions in America and France, gathered momentum leading up to the insurrection in Ireland of 1798. On 31 January 1793, to take one example, the *Ennis Chronicle* published as its front page a letter, from "An English Freeholder," entitled "Equality, no Liberty, or Subordination the Order of God, and the Welfare of Man":

> The favourite cry of the day is for Liberty. Let any man in these kingdoms shew me the slave, the single person who is not protected from tyranny and violence, the human being who cannot claim and find the protection of just and equal laws. Liberty is taken from none, but those, who, in some sense, are trampling upon others.—Every man in this country hath as much liberty as he can enjoy, confidently with his own good and the good of all about him. If he would have more liberty than this, he deserves to be considered as a tyrant and traitor to mankind.

The text, and the sentiment, is English in origin; in Ireland, even those unconvinced by abstract celebrations of liberty knew that these sentiments did not quite translate into an Irish context, though clearly the unionist editors of the *Ennis Chronicle* felt as though the people of the county might be suggestible. Our English freeholder is rowing against the more radical currents of enlightenment; he

Michael Griffin

seems also to be working against the enlightenment of Brian Merr-
iman, who complains:

> Mar d'imigh gach díth ar chríochaibh Fáil.
> Gan sealbh gan saoirse ag síolrach seanda,
> Ceannas i ndlí ná cíos ná ceannphoirt,
> Scriosadh an tír is níl 'na ndiaidh
> In ionad na luibheanna acht flíoch is fiaile,
> An uaisle b'fhearr chum fáin mar leaghadar
> Is uachtar lámh ag fáslaigh shaibhre
> Ag fealladh le fonn is foghail gan féachaint
> D'fheannadh na lobhar 's an lom dá léirscrios.
> Is dochradh dubhach, mar dhiú gach daoirse,
> Doilbheadh dúr an dúcheilt dlíthe,
> An fann gan feidhm ná faighidh ó éinne,
> Acht clampar doimhin is loighe chum léirscris,
> Falsacht fear dlí is fachnaoide airdnirt,
> Cam is calaois, faille is fábhar,
> Scamall an dlí agus fíordhath fannchirt,
> Dalladh le bríb, le fís, le falsacht. (Ó Murchú 1982, 21)

> [Without exception every man-jacks
> Up in arms that Ireland's bandjaxed:
> Farms are bankrupt, freedom banned,
> No law or leader in the land;
> Our country's raped and Luck, the coward,
> Shuns a virgin that's deflowered—
> Far a field our men are shipped
> While by grabbing hands she's stripped
> And as, powerless, we watch,
> All her beauty they debauch.
> But still there is the final curse—
> Lack of redress. What could be worse

Two Enlightenments of Merriman's County Clare

Than seeing one you love undone
And being forced to watch the fun?
They scorn our laws and ape our cries,
Promise the world—but it's all lies;
Right is guyed with mocks and gibes
And hangs there—its mouth stuffed with bribes.] (lines 75–92)

Merriman's voice, thus, is for Liam de Paor "a voice of the enlight-
enment of the people, an assertion of the new democracy that was
beginning to rise against absolutist Europe" (1998, 63). Though their
poetry chimed with a broader call for increased democracy, Merriman
and his contemporaries writing in Irish in eighteenth-century Clare
wrote aslant of the mainstream. The vernacular energy of *Cúirt an
Mheán Oíche* suggests that the local understanding of freedom was not
necessarily, or only, about the dissemination of the writings of Rous-
seau, Diderot, or Paine, nor was it necessarily or only about drawing
sustenance from the American Revolution, though these influences
and imperatives were all felt in Merriman's time and place. This was
freedom construed from below, not led from the top down by met-
ropolitan intellectuals: freedom to generate and sustain communities
too long constrained by alien and arbitrary systems of government,
distinction, and morality. This vernacular enlightenment is more com-
plex, and more difficult to document, than the enlightenment of print
culture. But a sense of the contemporaneity of print culture and the
manuscript culture of Irish-language writing in Merriman's Clare pro-
vides us with a compelling glimpse of the poem's context and origin.

Around the time of the appearance of *Cúirt an Mheán Oíche,*
an Ennis school, or court, of Irish-language poetry, instigated by the
radical poet and schoolmaster Tomás Ó Míocháin, assembled at Toi-
realach Ó Briain's home. It is likely that Brian Merriman attended
this school of poetry. Merriman and Ó Míocháin knew of each other

and each other's work—four of Ó Míocháin's poems can be found in Merriman's manuscript volume, housed in Cambridge University Library, England. Ó Míocháin's court was probably of immense benefit to Merriman as he honed his poetic gift; it was a forum that allowed him, as Brian Ó Dálaigh has remarked, to "meet and interact with like-minded individuals, to borrow Gaelic manuscripts and to have his own work assessed and circulated" (2000, 116).

Both Merriman and Ó Míocháin were teachers of mathematics, and both were unhappy with the denuded and depressed state of the country. These were lower-middle-class Catholic entrepreneurs. Together, they represent a disenfranchised stratum; educated and incisive, they articulated a grievance against English misrule in Ireland: against the crushing iniquities of the legal system, against the cruel economic imperatives for migration and emigration, against rack-renting and the social evils of absentee landlordism. But it was not just the imposition of an alien, abusive political system that was at fault; in Merriman especially, sexual constraints, arbitrarily imposed from within the religious culture itself, were equally to blame for the thinning of the rural population and the denial of bodily pleasures. And so, in Merriman's poem, the local body politic is as mired and unhealthy as the physical body. *Cúirt an Mheán Oíche* draws implicitly on broader libertarian and libertine currents: in its libertarianism, it gives a democratic voicing of the plight of the lower orders; in its libertinism, it chimed with the seventeenth- and eighteenth-century literary traditions of celebrating the free exercise of the libido. In both, the poem proposes as a remedy for social ills the full application of sexual and political freedom.

The continental enlightenment was not inaccessible to those living in provincial Ireland, nor was the development of an Angloglot public sphere in Irish print culture without contributions from the Irish-language cultural world. Ordinarily Irish-language poets adapted to changing realities by writing in English when the occasion demanded and the pocket required. John Lloyd, a Limerick man who spent most of his life in Clare, was one such poet. A Jacobite poet in Irish and author of the first book published in Ennis, Lloyd had taught in Dunaha, Kilrush, and in Ó Míocháin's mathematics school in Ennis. Lloyd's appointment was ended prematurely by excessive drinking. He moved on to Tulla and eventually to Toureen, where he composed *A Short Tour; or, An Impartial and Accurate Description of the County of Clare, with Some Particular and Historical Observations* (published by the *Clare Journal*'s Busteed and Trinder in 1780) and where he was found dead by the side of the road not long after. In spite of their abortive educational collaboration, Ó Míocháin would subsequently finance, and write a poetic prologue for, Lloyd's *Tour:*

> Such copious Blessings, doubtless, my dear Lloyd,
> For ages past our peaceful Land enjoy'd;
> 'Till Fate adverse, this inauspicious Time,
> Has chang'd it's Luck the Custom and the Clime!
> And now, alas! we see it quite distress'd,
> By Taxes weak'ned and it's Trade repress'd!
> The tenant wreck'd, unable to pay Rent,
> The needy Landlord driving for Content;
> Some gen'rous Souls, that would distress assuage,
> Of Means bereft, or, in the Debtor's Cage;
> Pure Wit and Parts eclips'd and disresepected,
> Our native Tongue most shamefully rejected;
> A Tongue primitive, florid and Sublime,
> Of nervous Force in either Prose or Rhime.[1]

1. *A Short Tour; or, An Impartial and Accurate Description of the County of Clare, with Some Particular and Historical Observations* was printed for John

Michael Griffin

This piece is a strongly worded indictment of the economic context in which the Irish language was being starved of oxygen. And yet, it does not go as far, politically, as Ó Míocháin's manuscript poetry. Writing in Irish, Ó Míocháin is freer to celebrate the humiliation of the English in their colonial endeavors. His drinking song *Ar dTréigean Bhoston d'Arm Shasana, 1776,* celebrates General Howe's evacuation of Boston on 17 March 1776, an engagement in which George Washington commanded the besieging American Army (Ó Muirithe 1988, 84).[2]

The antiestablishment tones and materials of Ó Míocháin's writings fermented in tandem with the international enlightenment. But they were not fed into the county's emerging public sphere through the local print culture, even though this was an Angloglot culture to which some Irish-language poets would occasionally contribute. That print culture was generally politically conformist. As rebellion simmered toward century's end, the Clare newspapers became more quiescent. Transgressive and seditious sentiments, meanwhile, found their voice in the manuscript and song culture of the

---

Busteed and George Trinder in 1780. This text is more readily available as a reprint from Ballinakella Press (Lloyd 1986). Meehan's poem is dated 24 May 1779. Vincent Morley (2002, 2005) and Brian Ó Dálaigh (1993) have published excellent scholarly work on Ó Míocháin's politics and poetry. Morley's scholarship contextualises and annotates the works of Ó Míocháin and other Irish poets writing on the American Revolution. See also Liam de Paor's introduction in Ó Muirithe (1988).

2. See also Morley (2002, 111) where Ó Míocháin's lines are translated: "It's a joy and a pleasure to me that Howe and the English, are spent and destroyed for ever, and stalwart Washington, supporting, courageous, is at the helm and in command of his realm; behold the mercenaries screaming without a refuge or city, without troops, without ships on the sea, and by Halloween it's certain that the British boors, will be trapped and in the custody of Louis [XVI]."

Irish-language poets, a culture in which Merriman and Ó Míocháin could write freely and more subversively than in the mainstream enlightenment packaged for the Clare gentry. Enlightenment was alive and circulating in Clare, but it was an enlightenment broken into "polite" and, for want of a better word, "impolite" registers. The impolite and boisterous tones of *Cúirt an Mheán Oíche* are what gave it, and give it, such liberatory resonance.

Courting an Elusive Masterwork

Reading Gender and Genre in
Cúirt an Mheán Oíche/The Midnight Court

SARAH E. MCKIBBEN

Cúirt an Mheán Oíche/The Midnight Court is a hard text to pin down. It courts our attention with its dazzling wordplay and propulsively rhymed couplets but confounds our attempts at settled interpretation. How are we to parse its multidirectional mockery, its slippery, contending mix of parody and protest?[1] One might simply read and enjoy its musicality, exuberant wit, and sheer verbal superabundance, as the text ardently invites us to do. Or one might argue that definitive explication of parody's indeterminacy and polyvalence is a mirage. If our judgments about the text are necessarily partial, though, our questions are no less pressing. We are left asking what to make of the text; how to situate it; who, what, when or indeed whether it critiques or compliments; and even what we are laughing at.

---

1. "Parody" may be broadly defined as an imitation of the style and stance of a literary text, author or tradition. See Falk and Teague (1993).

Courting an Elusive Masterwork

What cannot be disputed is the text's preoccupation with gender.[2] *Cúirt an Mheán Oíche* centers on a heated debate in opposing monologues between a woman and a man, who speak *for* women and men respectively, regarding a key aspect of gender (sexual and marital relations, addressed in intimate detail), in front of a special court composed of women, with a female judge. In response, many critical readings have focused on the text's alleged attitude toward women, often abstracting particular moments or aspects of the text to read as emancipatory and protofeminist or as conservative and androcentric. Rather than asking how a blatantly fanciful poem featuring a fairy court, a queen, and a twenty-foot-tall bailiff does or does not represent actual women, it seems more fruitful to consider how gendered discourse functions in the text as a whole. In so doing, we should bear in mind that the language of the court does not only represent things in the conventional sense, by referring to ideas, objects and events, like marriage, folk cures for singles, and women's dress. Through its verbal, thematic, and formal echoes it simultaneously refers parodically to other genres and thus to other ideological constructs, which in turn are intimately tied up with constructs of gender, as will become clear once we turn to examining *Cúirt an Mheán Oíche* in closer detail.

The poem begins with a framing prologue in which the speaker describes his custom of strolling in the lush countryside. The past habitual tense denotes his former habit, as he presently composes poetry instead of walking, while subtly conferring the authority of experience on his confident scene painting, as he joins his male poetic peers in authoritatively claiming the bucolic landscape he

---

2. "Gender" refers to the shifting and highly political sociocultural organization of sexual difference (itself understood as constructed and variable).

surveys. The past habitual tense of the first twenty-two lines also conveys the familiar and unexceptional, even canonical, quality of the pastoral mode in which he confidently writes (Kiberd 2000).

However, the speaker shortly succumbs to the heat and his own rhythmic if potentially vapid verse to fall asleep alongside some trees, no longer in command but unconscious and vulnerable. That the text is framed as a dream following a ramble in nature aligns it with the most prominent of the formal poetic genres of the period: that of the *aisling,* or allegorical vision poem. In the formal, prophetic incarnation of the genre, a solitary, typically male poet falls asleep at home or outside by a river or wood. He is found by a beautiful but distraught *spéirbhean* or sky-woman, whom he describes in courtly fashion with a concatenation of highly conventionalized, praiseful adjectives. He asks the woman her name and identity. She reveals that she is Ireland, deserted by her rightful spouse, the exiled Stuart king (by 1780 a lost cause, though still a source of resonant imagery), and left to suffer from national injustices that she enumerates before giving a prophecy of the leader's return to rescue her and return her lost sovereignty. At this point the poet usually awakes and despairs to find himself alone in the Ireland of the status quo (Ó Buachalla 1996).

By contrast, in *Cúirt an Mheán Oíche,* the poet's sleep is rocked by the arrival of a mud-spattered, gap-toothed, hideous Amazonian bailiff some twenty feet tall, well adorned with bumptious adjectives, who summons him to a fairy court of women. This is not the weak, alluringly disheveled woman of decorous contemporary poetry but "An mhásach bholgach tholgach thaibhseach, / Chnámhach cholgach dhoirrgeach ghaibhdeach" ("A hellish, hairy, haggard hank, / Bearded, bony, long and lank"; lines 47–48). The bailiff's grotesque and terrifying appearance, language, and behavior initiate a parody of the settled conventions of the typical eighteenth-century *aisling.*

Instead of passively awaiting rescue while elegantly bemoaning her lot like the usual *spéirbhean* (Ó Tuathaigh 1978), the bailiff loudly proclaims her outrage "Go doirrgeach d'fhoclaibh dána" ("with a gruff and angry shout"; line 61), brandishing a huge phallic staff at the overwhelmed and prostrate man, who can only listen, cowering before her threats of physical punishment.

The legal structure of trial and testimony inaugurated by the bailiff also heralds another genre entirely: the *barántas* or "warrant," a legalistic satire with the poet as summoner of the perpetrator of a petty crime for trial and punishment (Welch 1996, 32). This genre is itself inflected in *Cúirt an Mheán Oíche* with the tropes of an earlier legalistic literary form, that of the medieval Court of Love, in which love complaints were imaginatively adjudicated, which is in turn animated by the complaints common to yet another genre, that of the *chanson de la malmariée* (the song of the unhappily married woman) (Ó Tuama 1995, 68; Ó Murchú 2005). In effect, the *aisling* for which the opening prepares us is immediately disrupted and dislocated by these other forms, losing its generic coherence and primacy. Similarly, the initially confident and masterful narrator-poet persona finds himself unexpectedly dragged off to a fairy court to face trial and thereby effectively dragged into another genre (or three!), becoming dislodged from his accustomed verbal authority and virtually silenced for much of the rest of the poem.

Notwithstanding Merriman's generic gymnastics, the parody necessarily echoes elements of the *aisling* proper. The bailiff's loathsome appearance recalls the haggard old woman who embodied sovereignty in the medieval antecedents of the modern *aisling*. Her elemental quality evokes the nation, too, her mantle dragging in the mud as if she has just emerged from the primordial ooze, an earth-woman instead of a sky one. Her arrival likewise suggests an archaic indigeneity, being framed as part of the return of the fairies, ancient denizens of Ireland, to reassert their authority and fix what's gone wrong with the country. Most obviously, like the fairy woman of the *aisling,* who addresses the national crisis of lost sovereignty and collective oppression, the bailiff indicts lack of freedom, insecure tenure, and the unfair justice system. She proffers the fairy court as an alternative, saying, "Ní cúirt gan acht gan reacht gan riail, / Ná cúirt na gcreach mar chleacht tú riamh" ("This is no court where the law is bent / Like the courts of graft that you frequent"; lines 65–66).

Yet no sooner does she articulate those familiar legal complaints than the bailiff derails them to focus on one glaring emergency: the case of nubile women deprived of spouses, which threatens the survival of the supposedly depopulating nation (something that was not in fact the case) (O'Neill 1984). With this abrupt shift, *Cúirt an Mheán Oíche* subverts the sovereignty motif, refined locution, and millenarianism of the *aisling* by turning to the intimate, local, immediate concerns of the *malmariée,* expressed with gusto and blithe vulgarity. Where the *aisling* puts "foreigners" on trial, *Cúirt an Mheán Oíche* employs the refashioned structure of the *barántas* to put the narrator-poet—otherwise an author of the *aisling* genre and authority of the *barántas*—in the dock. It sends up the representation of collective national despair and vulnerability symbolized by the nation as a despairing woman deprived of her rightful spouse; instead, in *Cúirt an Mheán Oíche,* women are collectively frustrated without proper partners and ready not only to seize the sexual initiative but to take violent punitive action against unsatisfactory men (Ó Crualaoich 1983).

The poem thus hybridizes and burlesques the preeminent poetic genre of the era, in so doing both eroding the "authority of allegorical personification as a trope of mastery" (Bogel 2001, 126) and challenging the "one-sided seriousness of the lofty direct word"

Bakhtin 1981, 55). Where the *aisling* assumes (or affects) the limpid alignment of its parts, untroubled generic conventions, longstanding literary preeminence, and adequacy of poetic and political representation, its undoing deflates such confident or exclusive mastery. The *aisling,* it seems, is far from capturing the whole of the nation's preoccupations and far from immune to challenge, as not only Merriman's text but a rich panoply of eighteenth-century parodic literature in Irish demonstrates.

There are further implications to the parody. Where the *aisling* projects the Catholic nation's collective shame, oppression, and enfeeblement onto the gender-normative figure of the female Ireland, reciprocally augmenting the heroism of the longed-for Jacobite exiles abroad, *Cúirt an Mheán Oíche* does the reverse. By making women fierce, strong, and more than a little terrifying in their thwarted sexual longing, it relentlessly points up the sexual cowardice and incapacity of Irish men. *Cúirt an Mheán Oíche* punctures the image of masculine prowess promised by the *aisling*—always somewhat dubious given that the men of Ireland had yet to rescue their heroine or recover that lost sovereignty. The poem also unmasks the figure of the poet-rake seen triumphantly seducing all the women he meets in the more lighthearted "love" *aisling,* dismissing such claims as nothing but "maíomh" ("braggadocio"; line 935). Merriman's poem parodically revisits the once-fraught question of Irish emasculation under colonial domination— the unspeakable subtext of the *aisling*—not as trauma but as farce.

If prototypical, idealized nationalist manhood is a hollow shell, communal identity is rendered exaggeratedly inadequate, "fallen," and inevitably compromised. Instead of embracing a masterful, unsullied, culturally pure—and always receding or anticipatory— masculinity of national literary fantasy, the poem holds up an illegitimate, impure, antipatriarchal emblem instead. In celebrating the bastard as superordinately healthy and virile in the second monologue, the poem poses hybridity and not purity as a source of cultural, literary-linguistic, and communal strength. This contrasts with the pretense of an enduring binary opposition between us and them, native and foreign, seen in more "official" political poetry. At a time when absolute cultural distinctions were harder to sustain given the interpenetration of cultures and languages (Ó Dálaigh 2000)—and in contrast to the old image of colonialism as a rape that introduces miscegenation into "native" society—*Cúirt an Mheán Oíche* thinks differently, playfully envisioning transgression as potentially positive and fruitful, or at least comically undoing the longstanding force of a cultural taboo against the mixed identities that were already being lived.

We might also see the bastard as the equivalent of daredevil outsider poets like Merriman, who did not descend from a traditional poetic family, so that in celebrating such illegitimacy Merriman also trumpets his own insurgent muse and generically mixed poetic intervention (Ó Dálaigh 2000, 114).[3] However dominated men (and poets) appear to be within the dream world of the fairy court, they are hardly undone by the poem per se. Indeed, probably crafted for the delectation of the East Clare literary fraternity at a predominantly male *cúirt éigse* or poetic court (Ó Dálaigh 2000, 113), *Cúirt an Mheán Oíche* shows Merriman successfully holding court. As hyperbolically abjected as manhood is within the court, it is surely recuperated through this virtuoso poetic performance, with male prowess relocated to the arena of linguistic production. Similarly, the poet escapes from judgment and out of his dream,

---

3. Ó Dálaigh (2000) disputes the oft-repeated claim that Merriman was himself illegitimate.

recovering the authorial control and completeness that he never in fact lost. Indeed, his control seems the more confident in feigning incapacity. Lest this appear too neat, we might note in closing that the distinctly untriumphant ending underscores the text's quick-footedness in escaping from policing of any kind, as it refuses to answer any charges but requires the critical pursuit to continue.

Approaching *Cúirt an Mheán Oíche/The Midnight Court*

BRÍONA NIC DHIARMADA

*O*ne of the most challenging aspects of a text like Brian Merriman's ribald eighteenth-century masterpiece *Cúirt an Mheán Oíche/The Midnight Court* is determining how to read it as twenty-first-century readers. This issue is particularly pertinent for those who approach the poem in translation. It is commonplace now in literary studies to acknowledge that no reading is neutral; we, as readers and critics, bring to each text our own particular expectations, experiences, and prejudices. This is not to say that these may not be confounded by our engagement with the text, forcing us to look anew not only at the text but at our whole understanding of the *condition humaine*. And it is for this very experience that many of us turn to literature. Indeed, it is often a text's ability to achieve this feat that allows us to define it as a piece of world literature.

Cúirt an Mheán Oíche is, I believe, such a text. Since its composition in County Clare at the end of the eighteenth century, Merriman's poem continues to delight, amuse, and confound its many readers in equal measure. Why is this so? The poem, written in what was to become a minority language and outside the metropolitan centers that so often dictated taste, would grip the imagination of the local audience of the time and also manage to traverse the worlds of oral and literary transmission (Buttimer 2006, 320).

In the early 1900s, more than one hundred years after its composition, *Cúirt an Mheán Oíche* was on the lips of local farmers in Feakle, County Clare, memorized and recited word for word in the original Irish, even though the area, long associated with Merriman and his poem, was well along the road of language change from Irish to English. The esteem in which Merriman's verses were held is evidenced by their tenacity and their grip on the imagination of the local populace. It was not an uncommon occurrence for the work of poets to be remembered and preserved in their own locality, particularly later poets such as Máire Bhuí Ní Laoghaire in West Cork or the songs of Anthony Raftery or Colm de Bhailís in Connaught, whose work was preserved mainly as part of the song tradition. *Cúirt an Mheán Oíche,* however, also belonged to the literary manuscript tradition. Merriman himself was, of course, a literate poet, part of a literary coterie of Irish-language poets in County Clare and the surrounding areas. Even though *Cúirt an Mheán Oíche* was publically recited at public gatherings such as the *cúirteanna filíochta* (courts of poetry) or in local taverns or at fair-day assemblies, during Merriman's lifetime numerous manuscript versions of his poem were in circulation, as they later were throughout the nineteenth century. The poem also spawned numerous translations in English that continue to bring it to the attention of a wider audience.

Merriman's poem survived not only a change in the dominant language, but changes in taste and political upheaval. It survived to become a set text in the Irish-language curriculum in the schools of the newly independent Irish state founded in 1922. *Cúirt an Mheán Oíche* remained a fixture on the school curriculum from the 1920s until at least the 1970s, when the Irish-language school syllabus underwent radical change and simplification. It seems a little ironic to note that it was during what were the more liberal years—in terms of sexual morality—of the 1970s that the poem ceased to be a fixed text for examination. This sense of irony is increased when we consider that it was taught throughout the highly conservative years of the Free State and of what is often referred to as De Valera's Ireland, although its removal from the school curriculum (though not from the canon) had more to do with students' growing linguistic inability to deal with what Ciarán Carson has called Merriman's "intricate Irish" than any objection to theme and content (2005).

It is also ironic, in light of the above, that when Frank O'Connor, a particularly effective gadfly to the upholders of the socially and sexually repressive milieu of the Ireland of his time, published his own translation in 1945, it was promptly banned by the official state Censorship Board. The irony here is lessened, if only slightly, when we remember that the original poem was not set in its entirety. This is understandable given that it runs to just over a thousand lines, although the choice of extract was, not surprisingly, quite clearly dictated by content. What is surprising is that a poem that deals with subject matter as openly licentious as O'Connor's English version was clearly felt to be, ever made it anywhere near schoolchildren in the first place. The extract chosen and the one most often anthologized and learned by rote by thousands of schoolchildren was the opening passage, praised by the eminent scholar Eleanor Hull as "one of the most beautiful in Irish literature" (1913, 152). In it, Merriman describes and praises the beauties of *Loch Gréine* (Lough Graney), where he is wont to walk. What is most interesting about these four lines and the opening passage in its entirety, is not the originality of the descriptions, which, with due respect to Eleanor Hull, might well be described as generic pastoral: the sun shines, the ducks float by with a swan for company, the birds sing, the fawn frolics. Rather what gives this opening passage its power and its importance in the greater scheme of things has to do with form, in particular Merriman's use of the couplet as "metrical norm." This form, according to Seamus Heaney, rather than any originality or particular technique, gives the poem what he calls "its distinctive music." These opening lines, he writes, "establish a melody. They strike a tuning fork and immediately a whole orchestra of possibility comes awake in the poet's ear and in the language itself. Another great unfettered event gets under way" (1995, 52). The "unfettered nature" of Merriman's language and imaginative powers come more intensely into relief as the poem progresses. Having established his melody, Merriman goes full speed ahead as he introduces the grotesquely over-the-top burlesque figure of the female bailiff, who not so much punctures as entirely explodes the poet's slumber and the peaceful vista previously described.

It is easy to imagine how this description's slapstick nature would have been appealing in the classrooms of mid-twentieth-century Ireland. Merriman's descriptive powers are underpinned by the immense vitality and extravagance of the language and the word music that, although mimicked in translation, are particularly audible in the original Irish. Both these factors appealed quite clearly also to Merriman's original audience, including his peers in the Irish-language literary coteries of Ennis and East Clare, whose appreciation was undoubtedly heightened by the recognition of the deliberately parodic and subversive nature of Merriman's verses. Their enjoyment of Merriman's description of the bearded lady who awoke him from his sleep would have undoubtedly been heightened by their familiarity with the stock figure of the *spéirbhean* (or personification of Ireland as a beautiful young woman) of the conventional *aisling*. Merriman's hilarious send-up of what might be described as the defining genre of Irish-language verse in eighteenth-century literature was particularly potent. By Merriman's day, the *aisling* as practiced in the early years of the eighteenth century by figures such as Aogán Ó Rathaille had become a genre that had outlived its imaginative usefulness, the Jacobite politics that had inspired it having become outmoded and outdated by events. Although poems in the mode of the *aisling* continued to be composed into the nineteenth century, they were both in form and content imitative and insipid at best. Merriman, however, derived new vitality from the genre with his highly subversive engagement and mediation of the form not only in his burlesque caricature of the figure who jolts him from his reverie: "acht dúirt go doirrgeach d'fhoclaibh dána / 'Múscail, corraigh, a chodlataigh ghránna'" / "With a gruff and angry shout / 'Get up', she snarled, 'you lazy lout'" (lines 61–62), but also with what might be seen as a more fundamental subversion and rewriting of the genre by shifting the terms of reference from the battlefields of what might be described as national and anticolonial politics to those of sexual and gender politics.

The figure of the bailiff is not an exact parody of the *spéirbhean* but includes a sideways swipe, also, at some of the more self-regarding and pompous quasi-legal trappings such as the *barántas* (warrant) much loved by the *cúirteanna filíochta* (courts of poetry), as well as a sally in the direction of the legal system of the day. The bailiff's criticism of the flawed nature of the colonial courts is the closest the poem gets to political critique or indeed social realism, although to use the word "realism" in relation to *Cúirt an Mheán Oíche* is perhaps carrying things a little too far. The bailiff summons the poet to a sitting of a court that has been convened in Moygraney at the fairy fort under the auspices of "Munster's friend and Craglee's queen / Aeval, of heart and spirit clean" (lines 117–18). Aoibheall (anglicized Aeval) was the fairy queen of Munster, a figure who could be said to be synonymous with the much earlier figure of the Goddess of Sovereignty or titulary goddess. This was the female personification of sovereignty, which represented the land itself to whom, in the gendered cosmology of Early Ireland, the rightful king was wed, thus ensuring the fertility of the land and proper and peaceful relations. If the king's role is usurped, however, disaster results for the land and its people. And the political *aisling* of the late seventeenth and eighteenth centuries was a recasting, in the political terms of the times, of this founding mythos of early Gaelic society. It is interesting to see how Merriman retains or indeed returns to the underlying mythos while dispensing with the political and specific Jacobite accretions of the *aisling*. The cause for "the country's crisis" where, the bailiff tells us, "farms are bankrupt, freedom banned / no law or leader in the land" (lines 77–78) is not the usurping of the role of the rightful king but that gendered relations themselves are out of synch. Thus, the cause for the perilous state of affairs then current, according to the court, was not the political dispensation or the defeat of the old indigenous Gaelic order, nor was the cure the return of the rightful (Stuart) king of the *aisling*. Rather the problem was that there was a failure on behalf of the men of the country to procreate, leaving the women in a parlous state of frustration and the country itself on the brink of collapse (lines 98–103). That this had attendant and particular implications for the poet now being summoned to appear is left in no doubt (lines 106–16).

We have now reached in both stylistic and thematic terms the meat of *Cúirt an Mheán Oíche*. The poem then continues by way of three monologues: a young woman tells a tale of sexual frustration on her own behalf and on that of women generally; in the second we hear "a spirited and somewhat salty speech on behalf of the defence," as the introduction delicately puts it spoken, by "a wizened old josser" (line 358)—old Snarlygob, in Frank O'Connor's translation—who includes what Ciarán Carson has called "a paean to bastardy" (2005); the third consists of the young woman's angry riposte and a plea for the end of clerical celibacy before Aoibheall rises to give her judgment, after which the poem finishes as the poet awakens before his punishment is carried out. This denouement, some critics have argued—to paraphrase Eliot—ends not so much with a bang as a whimper, particularly in light of the almost run-away vigor and extravagance of the build-up.

But it is the tone and tenor of the main body of the poem that caused Eleanor Hull, among others, to speak in rather pejorative terms of its "unpleasant subject matter and often coarse language." In her introduction to part 2 of *A Text Book of Irish Literature,* she stated categorically: "from the nature of its subject and treatment, it can never be widely read, and is quite unsuitable to the young" (1913, 150). However, she states with equal certainty that "it is undoubtedly a piece of sustained power, and is wrought with artistic skill of the highest order," going on to praise "the mastery of form and speech" (151). It is an original work, she tells us, "wrought with conscious art and skill" (152). This distinction between the subject matter and the artistic success of *Cúirt an Mheán Oíche* has been an enduring one among commentators. In a situation such as pertained in the formative years of the making of the canon of Irish-language literature in which Hull played a highly significant part, it was particularly pertinent. A short number of years previously, the debate about the suitability of the Irish language and its literature for inclusion as a subject in schools and universities was in full spate. Numbered among those opposed to the language was the then notable academic Dr. Atkinson, professor of Sanskrit and philology in Trinity College, Dublin, who together with his colleague, the provost of Trinity, Dr. Mahaffy, gave evidence before the Vice-Regal Inquiry into Irish and Intermediate Education. In his evidence, Dr. Atkinson drew the tribunal's attention to the "intolerably low literature" found in the language. "I would not let any daughter of mine study it," he averred. "No human being could read [that material] without feeling absolutely degraded by contact with it, and the filth he would not demean himself even to mention" (Gaelic League n.d.a, 18). He invited those members of the inquiry who wished to do so to come to his rooms in Trinity College, where he could furnish numerous examples. He neglects to mention whether *Cúirt an Mheán Oíche* would be among them, although given the numerous manuscript versions extant, it would seem likely.

Atkinson's slurs on Irish-language literature did not go unanswered, however. Douglas Hyde, one of the founders of the Gaelic League, made the main written submission to the inquiry contesting Atkinson's views. He retorted: "My own experience is, that the Irish-speaking population are infinitely more clean and less ribald in their language than the English-speaking population. . . . To insinuate that these people tell indecent stories or use indecent language is grotesque, and could only be done by an ignorant man, who does not know the conditions of life about which he speaks" (Hyde n.d., 18–19). And of course Douglas Hyde was far from ignorant of Irish-language literature and was surely aware of *Cúirt an Mheán Oíche*, as, undoubtedly, was Father Richard Henebry, one of the strongest advocates of cultural nationalism, who stated, "As a matter of fact, Irish literature holds no indecent material. As the Irish people were and are pure, so is their literature pure in its persistent spirit" (Gaelic League n.d.b, 21). And while indecency is in the eye of the beholder, it would be hard to contest the accuracy of the adjective "ribald" when describing much of the tone and tenor of *Cúirt an Mheán Oíche*.

It is probably fair to say that the above comments tell us more about the ideological prejudices and leanings of the speakers than about the literature of which they spoke. Still, it would be hard to argue with the rather sensible comment of Hull that perhaps one would not wish to read it with young schoolchildren. Yet *Cúirt an Mheán Oíche,* as we have seen, was from the beginning accepted into the canon and deemed suitable for inclusion in the school curriculum by people who would have shared Father Henebry's views on the purity of the "Gael" and their literature. This seemingly untenable position was achieved by sleight of hand. What was presented in school textbooks was, as we have seen, not so much the edited highlights but a highly selective abridgment that stripped the poem of its body both literally and metaphorically. The artistic mastery of Merriman could now be enjoyed by all, set alongside Augustan verse while being emasculated and entirely denuded of its life force, irony of ironies in light of its subject matter.

This peculiar double-think can also be seen—albeit to a lesser extent—in Daniel Corkery's comments in *The Hidden Ireland* (2004). As Seamus Heaney notes, Corkery's account of the poem, in his hugely influential (though later much-contested) 1924 work *The Hidden Ireland,* is "[f]airly eager to play down Merriman's send-up of clerical celibacy and his advocacy of unconstrained heterosexual activity between consenting adults." Rather than saluting these extravagances as fantastic possibilities to be savored in a spirit of hilarity and transgression, Corkery spoke with a certain primness of the poet's treatment of "curious questions" (Heaney 1995, 52). Corkery was, as Heaney puts it, "a propagandist of the new self-Gaelicising Irish Free State" and his fastidiousness in dealing with the central themes of *Cúirt an Mheán Oíche* is matched only perhaps by the glee with which that aspect of the poem was played up (if that is indeed possible!) by his political and cultural nemesis, Frank O'Connor, in his 1945 translation. Although diametrically opposed to each other, it is interesting to note that Corkery and O'Connor both proffer explanations for Merriman's choice and handling of his theme of sexual libertarianism. According to Corkery, although he does concede nativist elements, the "irreligious ideas" promulgated in the text derive from "foreign influence," particularly the views of Voltaire and Rousseau and Enlightenment writers. O'Connor concurs, albeit for very different reasons, having his "own provocative anti-puritanical agenda" designed, according to Heaney, "to taunt, to affront the prudes, and goad the censorship board" (1995, 56), which was part of O'Connor's "Hibernia-harrowing enterprise" (57). O'Connor, in fact unwilling to concede any intellectual worth in the Irish-language tradition, remade Merriman and indeed his poem in his own preferred image and likeness—as "an intellectual Protestant and disciple of Rousseau" (1945, 10). He construed the intellectual independence evident in the poem to be proof that the poem emanates from a Protestant intellectual agenda despite any evidence, external or textual, to that effect: "[t]he religious background of *The Midnight Court* is Protestant. . . . In *The Midnight Court,* he [Merriman] imitated contemporary English verse, and it is clear that he had resolved to cut adrift entirely from traditional Gaelic forms. . . . Intellectually, Irish literature did not exist. What Merriman aimed at was something that had never been guessed at in Gaelic Ireland; a perfectly proportioned work of art on a contemporary subject, with every detail subordinated to the central theme" (6). Such comments tell us more about Frank O'Connor than they do about Merriman and indeed the same can be said of Daniel Corkery's rather more mealy-mouthed if less fanciful efforts.

The desire to codify and to trace literary influences and antecedents was and continues to be widespread in Merriman scholarship. Some scholars such as Seán Ó Tuama (1995, 63–77) and Máirín Ní Mhuirgheasa (1951, 7) have concentrated on European influence, seeing clearly the influence of medieval texts such as *Le Roman de la Rose* and the *Chanson de la Malmariée*. Some critics have seen the influence of Richard Savage's poem "The Bastard," published in Dublin, as well as those who draw parallels with Alexander Pope's "Rape of the Lock," or indeed see in Robbie Burns a kindred spirit. Others such as Gearóid Ó Crualaoich, however, emphasize the nativist elements, situating the court within the imaginative framework of the sovereignty myth reimagined as a personal vision by Merriman (Ó Crualaoich 1983, 95–104). Other readings have tended to emphasize the ethnographic. Liam P. Ó Murchú, editor of the definitive edition of Merriman's poem in Irish, makes the often attested claim that the poem is a critique of social conditions of the time by Merriman, in particular consciousness of the plight of women (Ó Murchú, 2005). However, the inaccuracy of the basis of the court's complaint, that the population was falling and that young people were not marrying, while in fact the opposite was the case, seems to make this kind of endeavor rather limiting although it has been argued by many that there is a note of realism in Merriman, as Heaney has pointed out that while "*The Midnight Court* has a demonstrable relevance to the Ireland of its day . . . it is hard to feel that Merriman wrote in a realistic spirit" (1995, 50).

One of the most interesting aspects of more contemporary commentaries has been the critics' attempt to present Brian Merriman as a proto-feminist and *Cúirt an Mheán Oíche* as a feminist text. The back cover of Patrick C. Power's (1971) translation published by Mercier Press announces: "This poem gives an excellent picture of rural Ireland in the late eighteenth century, and its feminism . . . makes it seem contemporary." Declan Kiberd, comparing *Cúirt an Mheán Oíche* with an earlier prose text, *Parliament na mBan* (The parliament of women), states: "As a male writer Dónal Ó Colmáin was speaking on women's behalf, just as a male poet Merriman, voiced the female protest against false gentility" (2000, 182–202), while Gearóid Ó Crualaoich believes that *Cúirt an*

Mheán-Oíche radically articulates the feminine side of the human psyche that is resident in women and men alike (1983, 95–104). On the other hand, Máirín de Búrca, a political activist speaking at the 1980 *Cumann Merriman* annual summer school, offended the sensibilities of the Merriman aficionados present by referring to the poem as nothing more than "sexist rubbish." The *Irish Times* reported on 29 August 1980 that "speakers from the floor reacted to Máirín de Burca's speech with some force, declaring that it was a poem well ahead of its time. Merriman was a poet, aware of women's sexuality and willing to discuss Irish sexual problems in an uninhibited fashion."

How then do we approach *Cúirt an Mheán Oíche*? With whom do we agree? Is it sexist rubbish or a liberating pro-woman masterpiece? Is it a work about gender relations? Is it a poem concerned with female sexual liberation at all or is it instead a work about male sexuality? Is it a child of the Enlightenment in Clare colors or a sophisticated psychosexual reimagination of the sovereignty myth? Is it a hugely original work or the reworkings of contemporaneous English or medieval French verse? The questions, contrasts, and permutations are endless—our response contingent on what we bring to the table. What is sure is that *Cúirt an Mheán Oíche,* this wonderful burlesque hybrid, this expression of the individual genius of Brian Merriman, this white-knuckled ride through linguistic rapids alive with the contrapuntal tones and counterpoint of human voices will continue to be read, to affront, to amuse, and to be a subject for debate for a long time to come.

Timeline of Events in America, Europe, and Ireland: 1770–1807

Year	America	Europe	Ireland
1770	Boston Massacre	Beethoven born Hegel born Captain Cook lands in Australia	
1773	Boston Tea Act		
1774	Coercive/Intolerable Acts Quebec Act First Continental Congress	Louis XVI succeeds to the French throne	
1775	Battles of Lexington and Concord		Daniel O'Connell born
1776	Declaration of Independence Howe evacuates Boston British capture New York Paine, *Common Sense*	Gibbons, *Decline and Fall of the Roman Empire* Smith, *Wealth of Nations*	Máire Bhuí Ní Laoghaire born
1777	Battle of Princeton Battle of Saratoga		
1778	Treaty of Alliance with France		Catholic Repeal Act: Penal Law Ban on intermarriage between Catholics and Protestants repealed The *Clare Journal* founded

93

Timeline 1770–1807

Year	America	Europe	Ireland
1780	American surrender Charleston (South Carolina) in Revolutionary War	The Gordon Riots result from a procession to petition parliament against the Catholic Relief Act *British Gazette and Sunday Monitor,* first Sunday newspaper in Britain, established	Merriman allegedly composes text
1781	Cornwallis surrenders to Washington at Yorktown (Virginia), fighting in the American Revolution ends	Kant, *Critique of Pure Reason*	
1782			Ireland obtains short-lived parliament Ban on Catholics studying abroad repealed Ban on Catholics teaching repealed
1783	Peace Treaty ends Revolutionary War Webster publishes *Blue-Backed Speller* Franklin, *Remarks Concerning the Savages of North America*	Pitt II becomes prime minister of England India Act gives Britain control in India	Royal Irish Academy founded
1784	The founder of the Shakers, Mother Ann Lee, dies.		*Ennis Chronicle* begins publishing Raftery born "Peep of Day Boys" founded in Armagh "Defenders" founded in Armagh
1785		Edmund Cartwright invents the power loom Hutton, *Theory of the Earth*	

Timeline 1770–1807

Year	America	Europe	Ireland
1786	Shay's Rebellion (Western Massachusetts)	Burns, *Poems, Chiefly in the Scottish Dialect*	J. C. Walker, *Historical Memoirs of the Irish Bards*
1787	Constitutional Convention		Daniel Thomas, *Observations* Merriman marries Kathleen Collins
1788	Constitution ratified African Americans found the First African Baptist Church in the United States	Bonnie Prince Charlie dies in France George III suffers first attack of "madness"	
1789	Olaudah Equiano, *The Interesting Narrative of the Life of Olaudah Equiano* Washington becomes president of United States	Outbreak of the French Revolution Bentham, *Introduction to the Principles of Morals* Blake, *Songs of Innocence* Edward Williams, *Barddoniaeth Dafydd ab Gwilym* Church property nationalized in France Lavoisier, *Elements of Chemistry*	Charlotte Brooke, *Reliques of Irish Poetry*
1790	Judith Sargent Murray, *On the Equality of the Sexes*	Burns, "Tam o' Shanter"	Máire Merriman born Sir Francis Nathaniel Burton serves as MP for Clare
1791	Vermont admitted to the Union	Paine, *The Rights of Man* Marquis de Sade, *Justine (The Misfortunes of Virtue)*	United Irishmen founded in Belfast
1792	Kentucky admitted to Union	Reign of Terror in France Wollstonecraft, *A Vindication of the Rights of Women*	Belfast Harp Festival The *Northern Star* newspaper established in Belfast

95

Timeline 1770–1807

Year	America	Europe	Ireland
1792		Wilhelm von Humboldt, *The Sphere and Duties of Government*	
1793	Fugitive Slave Act passed Whiskey Rebellion (Western Pennsylvania) Woolman, *A Word of Remembrance and Caution to the Rich*	France declares war on Britain and Ireland Louis XVI and Marie Antoinette executed Godwin, *Enquiry Concerning Political Justice*	Catholic Repeal Act: Law banning Catholics from Trinity College repealed
1794	Battle of Fallen Timbers against Native American Confederation	Fichte, *Wissenschaftslehre* Edward William *Poems, Lyric and Pastoral*	O'Connell returns from college at Douai (France) and admitted as lawyer at Lincoln's Inn (Dublin)
1795	Treaty of Greenville ends Northwest Indian War	French Directory	St. Patrick's seminary (Maynooth) founded *Bolg an tSoláir* Caitlín Merriman born Tadhg Gaelach Ó Súilleabháin dies
1796	Tennessee admitted to the Union John Adams elected president	Thomas Christian, *Pargys Caillit* (abridged Manx version of *Paradise Lost*) Edward Jenner creates a smallpox vaccination	Bunting, *A General Collection of the Ancient Irish Music* Orange Order established in Armagh French fleet attempts invasion at Bantry Bay (Cork)
1797			Merriman receives award for flax cultivation *Northern Star* suppressed
1798	Alien & Sedition Acts passed	Malthus, *The Principles of Population* Wordsworth and Coleridge, *Lyrical Ballads*	United Irishmen Rebellion "Year of the French" Battle of Vinegar Hill

Timeline 1770–1807

Year	America	Europe	Ireland
1798		Senefelder invents lithography	
1800	Seat of US government moves from Philadelphia to Washington DC Jefferson elected president		Union with Ireland Act (British Parliament)
1801	Jefferson inaugurated		Act of Union (Irish Parliament)
1802			Merriman moves to Limerick City
1803	Ohio admitted to Union Louisiana Purchase		Emmett's Rising, trial, and execution.
1804	Lewis & Clarke expedition begins	Napoleon becomes emperor of France	James Corocoran defeated in Wexford (February)
1805		Battle of Trafalgar	Merriman dies in Limerick City
1807		Slave trade abolished in the British Empire	Gaelic Society of Dublin founded

Glossary

Agallamh beirte: A traditional Irish-language oral art in the form of a poetic dialogue in which fluency of language, rhythm, and rhyming structures are paramount. The tone is usually humorous or satirical.

Aisling: A "vision poem," a poetic genre popular in Ireland in the seventeenth and eighteenth centuries closely linked with Jacobite politics. Typically the poet encounters a *spéirbhean*—a beautiful young woman—who promises the return of the exiled Stuart king, restoration of his reign, and a renewal of prosperity for both nation and poet.

Aoibheall: Pronounced "evil," anglicized as Aeval; the fairy queen and protector of the Dál gCais sept in County Clare. She is associated with the province of Munster and with Craglee (County Clare) in particular. "Her name meant 'sparkling' or 'bright' and reflects a common attribute of goddesses in ancient Irish culture. The twelfth century tract on king Brian Boru states that on the night before the battle of Clontarf, Aoibheall appeared to him and foretold he would be killed in that contest and that the first of his sons whom he would see on that day would succeed him as king. The post-medieval poets numbered Aoibheall as one of the principal otherworld women of Munster" (Ó hÓgáin 1991, 38). See also MacKillop (1998, 5). Aoibheall also appears in Donncha Ruadh mac Conmara's famous Irish-language poem, *Eachtra Ghiolla an Amaráin/ Adventures of a Luckless Fellow.*

99

Glossary

Bacchanalia: A religious festival honoring the wine god Dionysus/Bacchus and associated with drunken revelry. Initially restricted to women, men were later admitted in Roman times. Alcohol does not feature in *Cúirt an Mheán Oíche*. Frank O'Connor's translation was entitled a *rhythmical bacchanalia*.

Barántas: A literary genre framed as a legal warrant, or summons, that was usually humorous and witty. The offender, crime, judge, details of trial, and proposed punishment are discussed in bombastic style. Usually commences with the legalistic term *Whereas*. For further information see *The Oxford Companion to Irish Literature*, 1996. See also *An Barántas* and "The Poetic Warrant" (Ó Fiannachta 1978 and 1991).

Burns, Robert (1759–96): The best-known poet to have written in the Scots language. Regarded as a pioneer of the Romantic Movement.

Chaplinesque: Referring to British-born silent movie star, Charlie Chaplin (1889–1977) and his innovative comedic style.

County Clare: One of the six counties of the province of Munster. The others are Cork, Kerry, Limerick, Tipperary, and Waterford.

Court of Love Poetry: Medieval European poetic convention distinguished between erotic love and spiritual attainment. Courtly love poetry viewed women as an ennobling spiritual and moral force, but this view contradicted ecclesiastical sexual attitudes. Such poets praised romantic love as the highest good in contrast to clerics who considered romantic and sexual love as sinful. From 1100 to 1300 A.D., such love poetry prevailed in the courts of England and Europe.

Courts of Love: Medieval troubadours describe such courts as deciding affairs of the heart and determining rights and wrongs of lovers' lives. Tribunals of ten to seventy women heard cases of love and passed judgment based on the "rules of love." Nineteenth-century historians accepted their existence, but later historians question this presumption.

Courts of Poetry: See *Cúirt Éigse.*

Craglee: Anglicized form of Léithchraig, the reputed home of Aoibheall, the fairy queen of Munster, in folk belief. See MacKillop 1998.

Cratloe: Anglicized form of Creatlach, a village and townland in the parish of Kilfintinan, barony of Bunratty Lower, on the road from Feakle to Limerick city.

Cúirt(eanna) Éigse (Court[s] of Poetry): As was common in eighteenth-century Munster, poets convened in a public venue for annual or biannual meetings that often coincided with holy days or fair days. At such gatherings poets performed new compositions and exchanged manuscripts. Established poets received validation while younger poets sought recognition. David Dickson suggests, "Their rituals seem to have been inspired less by the old bardic schools than by the formal procedures of the quarter sessions, the court 'president' acting like a presiding magistrate. But what was important about these events was that in the absence of upper-class or institutional patronage and with the fragmentation of the traditional literary families, they conserved a vestigial esprit de corps among the heterogeneous collection of schoolmasters, priests, land agents and well-to-do farmers who participated, helping to maintain standards of literary knowledge among the Irish-language writers and fostering a spirit of convivial egalitarian emulation" (Dickson 2005, 262).

Cumann Merriman: Founded in 1967 and named in the poet's honor. Through its annual summer and winter schools, Cumann Merriman promotes interest in the poet and the history and traditions of Thomond. It fosters all aspects of Irish culture. See http://www.merriman.ie/index.en.

Glossary

Doorus: Anglicized form of Dúire, a townland in the parish of Feakle overlooking Lough Graney near where Merriman lived.

De Valera, Éamon (1882–1975): Former *Taoiseach* and president of Ireland. Considered the most important Irish politician of the twentieth century and often associated with conservative and protectionist cultural policies.

Enlightenment, The: An eighteenth-century movement advocating reason as the primary basis of authority. The Enlightenment stressed human reasoning and encouraged scientific thinking over blind faith and absolute obedience. Characterized by governmental consolidation, nation creation, and greater rights for common people, during the age referred to as "The Enlightenment," the absolute influence of hierarchical institutions such as the nobility and Church declined.

Ennis: Anglicized form of Inis, County Clare's principal town.

Feakle: Anglicized form of An Fhiacail, a parish in northeast County Clare forming the northeastern extremity of the county.

Fiannaíocht: Stories and literature about the *Fianna*, a band of semi-independent warriors that appear in Irish mythology where they feature in several stories (Fenian cycle) which describe the exploits of their leader Fionn mac Cumhaill and their efforts to defend Ireland from invaders.

Free love: A social movement promoting the rejection of marriage, which it views as social bondage enslaving women. Drawing on civil libertarian beliefs it rejects state and Church regulation of social behavior.

Ibrickane: Anglicized form of Íbh Breacáin, a coastal barony in west Clare, incorporating the parishes of Kilfarboy (Miltown Malbay) and Kilmurry Ibrickane. Merriman's family originated from this area.

Glossary

Jacobite: A follower of Jacobitism, the political movement dedicated to the return of the Stuart kings to the throne of England, Ireland, and Scotland from their exile in Europe. See *Aisling* and **Stuart.**

Kilbreckane: Anglicized form of Cill Bhreacáin, a townland in the parish of Doora, barony of Bunratty Upper on the primary Quin-Ennis road. Merriman would have passed through it on his way from Feakle into Ennis.

Libertarian: A political philosophy that has as a basic tenet the liberty of each individual to be sovereign over his or her body and the extension of such liberty to life and property.

Libertine: A person devoid of any restraints, frequently rejecting all religious norms, accepted sexual morals, and forms of behavior sanctioned by society.

Lough Graney: Anglicized form of Loch Gréine, a lake in northeast County Clare.

Moinmoy: Anglicized form of Cnoic Mhánmhaí, series of hills in the parish of Feakle.

Moy Grane: Anglicized form of Maigh Gréine, the plain overlooking Lough Graney/Loch Gréine.

Munster: A province that—along with Leinster, Ulster, and Connaught—is one of the four provinces of Ireland. Munster consists of six counties: Clare, Cork, Kerry, Limerick, Tipperary, and Waterford.

O'Connor, Frank (1903–1966): Cork-born author of numerous collections of short stories and translator of Irish-language poetry. His English-language version of *Cúirt an Mheán Oíche* was famously banned in 1945.

Glossary

Parl(i)ament na mBan/**The Women's Parliament:** A didactic text written in 1697 by Father Dónall Ó Colmáin for his pupil, James Cotter.

Piseog(a): An Irish language word often used in Hiberno-English. It refers to folk beliefs, charms, spells, and superstitions.

Quin: Anglicized form of Cuinche, a village, townland, and parish in the barony of Bunratty Upper in County Clare.

Rabelaisian: Referring to gross robust humor, extravagance of caricature, satire. Named for the sixteenth-century French Renaissance writer François Rabelais.

Spéirbhean: A female (literally, sky-woman) of considerable beauty associated with the *aisling* vision poetry. See **Aisling.**

Stuart: Family name of the kings who lost control of Ireland and Britain after the Williamite War culminating in the Battle of the Boyne (1690). The House of Stuart was the royal house of Scotland (from 1371) and of England (from 1603). It was restored to the throne in 1660 after the Commonwealth but ousted in 1714 when the House of Hanover seized the throne. The return of the Stuarts is a dominant trope in *aisling* poetry. See *Aisling* and **Jacobite.**

Teermaclane: Anglicized form of Tír Mhic Calláin/Tíortha Mhic Cuileáin, a small hamlet and townland in the parish of Killone, on the primary Ennis-Kildysert road.

Tradraighe: Anglicized form of Tradraí, part of the ancient territorial divisions of Thomond. Stretched from Bunratty on the river O'Garney in the east to the estuary of the river Fergus in the west of County Clare and containing the most fertile lands in the county.

Glossary

United Irishmen (Society of United Irishmen): An eighteenth-century liberal political organization established in 1791 to unite all Irishmen in the pursuit of universal male suffrage and to seek Parliamentary reform, it evolved into a revolutionary republican organization inspired by the French revolution. The United Irishmen were responsible for the 1798 Rebellion in Ireland.

Whereas: a legalistic term used to begin a *barántas*/warrant poem.

Partial Publication and Production History

The following list is intended to serve as a guide to the various editions, translations, versions, productions and interpretations of the text. Manuscript versions are not included.[1]

1844   *Limerick Reporter* (16 July 1844) publishes James McCurtin's partial translation of the poem's first section.

1850   John O'Daly (Dublin) publishes *Mediae Noctis Consilium: Poema Heroico-Comicum, quo Nihil aut Magis Gracile, aut Poeticum, aut Magis Abundans in Hodierno Hiberniae Idiomati Exolescit.* 32p.[2]

1879   Gill (Dublin) publishes *Noctis Consilium,* a reprint of O'Daly's 1850 edition. 32p. On O'Daly's death, Gill acquires remaining copies of 1850 publication and reissues it with a new title leaf.

1. The Vincent Dowling Archive at Kent State University contains a screenplay of *The Midnight Court.* Box 8, series 7, folder 66.

2. Possibly 1860. "D. J. O'D" cites David Comyn as a source for believing Daly's volume appeared in 1860. See *The Irish Book Lover* 3, no. 2:31.

Ludwig Christian Stern. From *Zeitschrift für
Celtische Philologie.*

1880   *The Irishman* publishes Donnchadh Ulf/Denis Woulfe's
            English verse translation.[3]

1893   Pádraig Ó Briain (Dublin) publishes *Mediae Noctis
            Consilium* by Briano Mac Gilla Meidhre. Sells at 1s, 6p. 43p.

3. T. F. O'Rahilly claims that Donnchadh Ulf/Denis Woulfe published an
alternative translation in an unidentified County Clare newspaper some years previ-
ously. See O'Rahilly 1912.

Publication/Production History

1897 Michael C. O'Shea privately prints two hundred copies in Boston, Massachusetts. 49p.

1905 L. C. Stern publishes *Cúirt an mheadhóin oidhche* with commentary, and German translation, *Der mitternächtige Gerichtshof*, in *Zeitschrift für Celtische Philologie*, vol. 5, pp. 193–415.

1909 Celtic Press (Dublin) publishes *Cúirt an Mheadhoin Oidhche/The Midnight Court* (school edition), edited and annotated by Rev. Canon F. W. O'Connell (Conall Cearnach). 32p. Sells at 6d.

1909 Shandon Publishing Company (Cork) publishes *Cúirt an Mheadhóin Oidhche*, an English translation of *The Midnight Court* by an "Intermediate Teacher."

1909 Pádraig Ó Briain (Dublin) republishes *Mediae Noctis Consilium*. 43p. Preface refers to 1893 edition as 1891.

1912 Hodges, Figgis (104 Grafton St., Dublin) publishes *Cúirt an Mheadhon Oidhche*, edited by Risteárd Ó Foghludha (Fiachra Éilgeach). 185p.

1922 Ristéard Ó Foghludha acquires charter that purportedly contains Merriman's biographical details.

1926 16 Sept. J. Cape (London) publishes *The Midnight Court and The Adventures of a Luckless Fellow*, an English verse translation by Percy Arland Ussher. Preface by W. B. Yeats, woodcuts by Frank W. Peers. 79p.

1926 Boni and Liveright (New York) publishes *The Midnight Court and The Adventures of a Luckless Fellow*, translated by Percy Arland Ussher. Black-and-white woodcuts by Frank W. Peers. 79p.

1928 Educational Company of Ireland (Dublin) publishes *Giotaí as Cúirt an Mheadhon-Oidhche maille le nótaí le Conall Cearnach*, edited by the Rev. F. W. O'Connell (Conall Cearnach). 38p.

Publication/Production History

1941 May. Frank O'Connor's English verse translation appears in *The Bell* (Dublin) 2, no. 2.

1945 Maurice Fridberg (Dublin) publishes *The Midnight Court: A Rhythmical Bacchanalia from the Irish of Bryan Merryman*, an English verse translation by Frank O'Connor. Black-and-white text decorations/illustrations by Hugh Stevenson. 61p. Sells at 6s.

1946 Subscription fund to erect a plaque in Feakle founders on technicality. Funds subsequently invested in new edition of text to be edited by Risteárd Ó Foghludha (Fiachra Éilgeach).

1946 Frank O'Connor's translation appears in *The Dublin Magazine* (Jan.–Mar.)

1946 3 May. Censorship Board (Ireland) bans O'Connor's translation.

1946 9 July. Censorship Board rejects appeal.

1947 BBC (Third) broadcasts O'Connor's translation on 14 and 19 Sept. Produced by W. E. Rogers, directed by Louis MacNeice. Cast includes Madge Herron and Frank O'Connor.

1949 Hodges, Figgis (Dublin) publishes *Cúirt an Mheadhón Oidhche*, edited by Risteárd Ó Foghludha (Fiachra Éilgeach). New edition. 48p. Sells at 10s 6d.

1949 Lord Longford (Frank Pakenham) publishes *The Midnight Court*, an English verse translation in *Poetry Ireland*, no. 6.

1949 Trumpet Books (Cork) publishes *The Midnight Court*, an English verse translation by Lord Longford (Frank Pakenham). Introduction by Pádraic Colum. 28p. Sells at 2/-.

1952 Brendan Behan completes an entire translation and recites it publicly in McDaid's Pub (Dublin), but loses the manuscript several days later in the Conservative Club, York St. (Dublin).

Publication/Production History

1953   The Dolmen Press (Dublin) publishes *The Fourth Part of The Midnight Court*. Six-page leaflet, with specimen pages, serves as prospectus for the book.

1953   23 May. The Dolmen Press (Dublin) publishes *The Midnight Court*, an English verse translation by David Marcus. This is a limited edition (200 copies) for subscribers. Woodcuts by Michael Biggs. 52p. Launched at Monument Café, 39 Grafton Street (Dublin).

1955   New Rochelle (New York) produces a sound recording of O'Connor's English verse translation read by Siobhán McKenna, produced and directed by Arthur Luce Klein. Sells at $5.95.

1956   29 Oct. The BBC (Third) broadcasts O'Connor's translation. Among performers are Cyril Cusack, Peg Monahan, and Adrienne Corri.

1957   As part of An Tóstal/Dublin Theatre Festival, An Compántas produces a late night bilingual production/ revue based on *Cúirt an Mheán Oíche/The Midnight Court* at the Pocket Theatre, Ely Place (Dublin). Cast includes: Séamus Kavanagh, Niall Toibín, Éamonn Ó Ceallaigh, and Con Lehane.

1958   A partial translation appears in Brendan Behan's *Borstal Boy*.

1958   25 Sept. The Lantern Theatre Club (Dublin) produces *Cúirt an Mheán Oíche*, a dramatic version of Arland Ussher's translation.

1959   Knopf (New York) publishes *Kings, Lords and Commons: An Anthology from the Irish*, containing a revised version of O'Connor's 1945 translation.

1961   11 July. Censorship Board (Ireland) bans *Kings, Lords and Commons*, as it contains O'Connor's previously banned translation of *Cúirt an Mheán Oíche*.

1961   8 Dec. Censorship Board revokes ban on O'Connor's *Kings, Lords and Commons*.

Publication/Production History

1961	Eoghan Ó Tuairisc's three-act play *Cúirt an Mhéan Oíche* wins first prize at An tOireachtas literary competition.
1962	Eoghan Ó Tuairisc's play *Cúirt an Mhéan Oíche*, inspired by Merriman's poem, is performed at The Damer (Dublin). Cast includes Pádraig Ó Gaora, Máire Ní Chonchradha, Breandán Ó Dúill, Diarmaid Ó hAirt, Barra Ó hUallacháin, Mairéad Ní Dhálaigh, Máirín Ní Dhuairc, and Nuala Ní Dhomhnaill. Produced and directed by Tomás Mac Anna.
1963	27 Dec. WNYC-FM radio (New York) broadcasts Siobhán McKenna reading Brian Merriman's *Midnight Court* on *Spoken Words* (55 min.)
1966	9 June. WNYC-FM radio (NY) broadcasts Siobhán McKenna reading Brian Merriman's *Midnight Court* on *Spoken Words* (55 min.).
1966	The Dolmen Press issues *The Midnight Court*, a new version of David Marcus's edition. Second edition. Woodcuts by Michael Biggs. 43p. Sells at 9s. 6d. (paperback), 21s (cloth).
1966	Raidió Teilifís Éireann produces *Cúirt an Mheán-Oíche* for television, directed by Louis Lentin. Filmed at Lough Graney and Jerpoint Abbey (Kilkenny). Cast includes Caitlín Maude and Fionnuala Ní Fhlanagáin. RTÉ submits it as one of two Irish entries in the Golden Harp Folk Festival, an international competition for television organizations.
1967	Cumann Merriman founded to commemorate Brian Merriman. Membership fee: two guineas. Committee: Micheál Ó hAodha, Brendan MacLua, Con Howard, Daithí Ó hUaithne, Seán Ó Tuama, Dónal Ó Foghlú, Ciarán Mac Mathúna, Séan Harrington, Tadhg MacConmara, and Kevin Vaughan.
1968	13–22 Sept. First Merriman Summer School. Fee: ten guineas.

Publication/Production History

1968   Merriman exhibition in the Ennis Museum, Ennis, County Clare.

1968   Preas Dolmen (Dolmen Press) (Dublin) publishes *Cúirt an Mheán Oíche*, edited by Dáithí Ó hUaithne. Introduction by Seán Ó Tuama. 56p.

1968   The Dolmen Press reissues David Marcus's translation, *The Midnight Court*. Third edition. 43p. Limited edition of five hundred copies.

1968   15. Feb. Éamon Keane performs *The Midnight Court* in English and Irish at the Chariot Inn, Ranelagh (Dublin). Event organized by Cumann Merriman.

1968   3 June–6 July. Gemini and Philip O'Brien present a musical entertainment based on Brian Merriman's *Midnight Court* by David Marcus and Séan McCann. A new modern version with songs adapted for the stage (adults only). Cast includes Eamon Keane, Arthur O'Sullivan, Maureen Toal, Bill Golding, May Cluskey, Vincent Smith, Liz Davis, Frank Kelly, Margaret Burke, and Eoin Ó Súilleabháin. Music by Shay Healy, set design by Alan Pleass. Directed by Michael Bogdanov.

1968   12 June. *Irish Times* publishes extracts from O'Connor's previously banned translation.

1968   14 July. Plaque honoring Merriman unveiled at Feakle by Patrick Hillery, Irish Government minister.

1969   Dolmen Press (Dublin) republishes *Cúirt an Mheán Oíche*, edited by Dáithí Ó hUaithne. Second edition.

1969   The Dolmen Press reissues David Marcus's translation.

1969   31 Jan. Liam Clancy and Séamus Ennis perform *The Midnight Court* in Nenagh (Tipperary).

1971   Mercier Press (Cork) publishes *The Midnight Court*, with the text in Irish and a facing English translation by Patrick C. Power. Cover design by John Skelton. 96p. Sells at 60p.

Publication/Production History

1972   The Dolmen Press reissues David Marcus's translation. Woodcuts by Michael Biggs. 43p.

1972   June. Heleana Carroll and Dermot McNamara perform *The Midnight Court* at the White Horse Tavern, Greenwich Village (New York).

1972   July. Scarrif Players Theatre Group (Clare) perform *The Midnight Court*. Cast includes: Alan Sparling, Caoimhín Jones, Marie Young, Anne Jones, Denise Sparling and Siobhán McGrath.

1972   Aug. Metamorphix performs a mime and ballet version of *The Midnight Court* at Trinity College, Dublin. Adapted by Carrol O'Daly, directed by Michael Sheridan, choreographed by Sylvia Behan, music by Dónal Lunny and Planxty. Cast includes Peter Caffrey, Susan Scott, Anne Hasson, Jean Byrne, Paul Brennan, Éamon O'Dywer, and Mary Lennon.

1972   Dec. The Dramatic Society, Queens University Belfast, performs *The Midnight Court* in Aquinas Hall.

1973   Mercier Press (Cork) issues a recording of Coslett Ó Cuinn/ Coslett Quin's *Midnight Court* (IRL 13). Music by James Lockhart and Charles O'Connor. Cast includes Joe Dowling, Éamonn Kelly, Fidelma Murphy, and Máire Ní Dhomhnaill.

1974   Dolmen Press (Dublin) republishes *Cúirt an Mheán Oíche*, edited by Dáithí Ó hUaithne. Third edition.

1974   May–June. Nora Relihan and Mary Deady perform a dramatization of *The Midnight Court* at Listowel Writers Week (Kerry).

1974   Folcroft Library Editions publishes Percy Arland Ussher's *Midnight Court and The Adventures of a Luckless Fellow*. Woodcuts by Frank W. Peers (reprint of 1926 edition published by Boni and Liveright). 79p.

1974   Haskell House Publishers (New York) publishes O'Connor's *Midnight Court: A Rhythmical Bacchanalia from the Irish of Bryan Merryman*.

Publication/Production History

1975   Dolmen reissues David Marcus's translation of *The Midnight Court*. Woodcuts by M. Biggs. 39p. Pocket-size edition sells at 60p.

1977   Mercier Press (Cork) republishes Power's *Midnight Court*, with the text in Irish and a facing English translation.

1977   Norwood Editions (Norwood, PA) publishes Percy Arland Ussher's *Midnight Court and The Adventures of a Luckless Fellow* (reprint of 1926 edition published by Boni and Liveright, New York). 79p.

1977   8 June. BBC Radio Three broadcasts O'Connor's translation. Cast includes Pauline Delaney, Kevin Flood, and Sean Barrett. Directed and produced by Mary Price.

1978   Dolmen Press (Dublin) republishes *Cúirt an Mheán Oíche*, edited by Dáithí Ó hUaithne. Fourth edition.

1978   R. West (Philadelphia) publishes Percy Arland Ussher's *Midnight Court and The Adventures of a Luckless Fellow*, (reprint of 1926 edition published by Boni and Liveright). Preface by W. B. Yeats and woodcuts by F. W. Peers. 79p.

1980   Wouter F. Pilger publishes *La Noktmeza Kortumo*, Albert Goodheir's Esperanto translation of the text. 36p.

1981   A partial translation by Thomas Kinsella appears in *An Duanaire 1600–1900: Poems of the Dispossessed*, edited by Seán Ó Tuama and Thomas Kinsella.

1981   July. Scarrif Players Theatre Group (Clare) performs a dramatization of *The Midnight Court* at the Belltable Theatre (Limerick city).

1982   An Clóchomhar Tta. (Dublin) publishes *Cúirt An Mheon-Oíche*, edited by Liam P. Ó Murchú. 117p.

1982   AMS Press (New York) publishes Percy Arland Ussher's *Midnight Court and The Adventures of a Luckless Fellow* (reprint of the 1926 edition published by Boni and Liveright). 79p.

Publication/Production History

<table>
<tr><td>1982</td><td>Mercier Press (Cork) publishes The Midnight Court, an English verse translation by Coslett Ó Cuinn. Illustrations by John Verling. 87p. Sells at £7.50. Special limited edition of three hundred copies signed by author and illustrator also available.</td></tr>
<tr><td>1982</td><td>Haskell House Publishers (New York) reissues O'Connor's translation. 48p.</td></tr>
<tr><td>1982</td><td>An Clóchomhar Tta. (Dublin) publishes Cúirt An Mheon-Oíche, a scholarly edition of the original Irish-language text by Liam P. Ó Murchú that includes Denis Woulfe's 1880 English translation. 117p.</td></tr>
<tr><td>1982</td><td>24–29 May. Dublin Shakespeare Society performs Celia de Fréine's translation and dramatization of The Midnight Court in The Studio, 50 North Great Georges Street (Dublin). Cast includes Martin Maguire, Helen Byrne, Brenda McSweeney, Orla Golden, Fiona Skehan, Michaele Traynor, Bríd Ní Chumhaill, Noëlle O'Reilly, Anne Byrne, Paul Fox, John Flood, Michael Clarke, Rory McCloskey, Annick Rolle. Music by Liam Ó Maonlaí and Nuala O'Sullivan. Set design by John Flood. Costume design by Reg Deane. Assistant director Willie Byrne. Director Celia de Fréine.</td></tr>
<tr><td>1982</td><td>5–11 Oct. John Verling exhibits illustrations for The Midnight Court at Caldwell Gallery (Dublin).</td></tr>
<tr><td>1983</td><td>Sept. Éamon Morrissey performs O'Connor's Midnight Court in Slane Castle (County Meath).</td></tr>
<tr><td>1983</td><td>July. Castle Players (Dundalk) tour Detroit, Chicago and New York with The Midnight Court.</td></tr>
<tr><td>1984</td><td>9–17 Oct. Abbey Theatre (Dublin) performs Cúirt an Mheán Oíche in the Peacock. Cast includes Bríd Ní Neachtain, Máire Ní Ghráinne, Peadar Ó Luain, Macdara Ó Fatharta, Áine Ní Mhuirí, Bairbre Ní Chaoimh, Máire Hastings, Peadar Mac Gabhann, Seán Campion, and</td></tr>
</table>

Micheál Ó Briain. Music by Dónal Ó Luinigh, production management by John Costigan and costume design by Wendy Shea. Directed by Siobhán McKenna. Seventeen performances.

1984   6 Oct. David Marcus performs his translation of *The Midnight Court* at the Temple Bar Studios, Essex Street (Dublin).

1985   The Brehon Press (Dublin) publishes *On Trial at Midnight: Cúirt an Mheán-Oíche/The Midnight Court*, Bowes Egan's English translation. Illustrations by Carolyn Mann. 44p.

1985   9 Mar. Carlow Little Theatre Society performs *The Midnight Court* at the Belltable Theatre (Limerick).

1985   Uilleam Nèill/William Neil publishes *Cùirt a'Mheadhain Oidhche*, a Scots-Gaelic translation in *Gairm*, 1 Mar. and 1 June.

1986   Hans-Christian Kirsch publishes *Das Mitternachtsgericht* (Mainz: Hempel), a German translation by Frederik Hetmann. Illustrations by Günther Stiller and an essay, "Die Barden vom Torffeuer," by Hetmann.

1986   Mercier Press (Cork) publishes *The Midnight Court*, third edition of Patrick C. Power's English and Irish text. 96p.

1986   Oct. Dolmen Theatre Company (Dundalk) performs *The Midnight Court* at drama festival in Muncie, Indiana.

1987   Mercier Press (Cork) reissues Coslett Ó Cuinn's *Midnight Court*. Illustrations by John Verling. 87p.

1988   An Gúm (Dublin) publishes *Cúirt na Gealaí: coiméide trí ghníomh*, Eoghan Ó Tuairisc's three-act, Irish-language dramatic and comedic adaptation. 63p.

1988   5 Jan. Éamon Morrissey performs O'Connor's *Midnight Court* on RTÉ Radio 1 as "play of the week."

1988   3–5 Dec. Najit Productions (London) performs a new adaptation of *The Midnight Court* at the Triskel Arts Centre (Cork).

Publication/Production History

1989   O'Brien Press (Dublin) publishes *The Midnight Court* (reprint of O'Connor's 1945 English verse translation). Illustrations by Brian Bourke. 72p.

1989   Poolbeg Press (Dublin) publishes *The Midnight Court*, David Marcus's dramatic script. 70p.

1989   Poolbeg (Dublin) publishes David Marcus's *Midnight Court and Other Poems translated from the Irish.*

1989   9 May. RTÉ Radio 1 broadcasts Éamon Morrissey reading O'Connor's 1945 translation.

1989   3 June–22 July. Mary McGuckian devises and directs *The Midnight Court* at the Project Theatre (Dublin). Cast includes Michael McElhatton, Nora Connolly, Joan Sheehy, Veronica Quilligan, Sean Lawlor, and Kate Binchy. Previously performed in Cork and London.

1989   24–28 July. Everyman Studio presents *The Midnight Court* in the Cork Arts and Theatre Club.

1989   22–24 Sept. Everyman Studio presents *The Midnight Court* in Bangor Little Theatre (Down).

1990   19–20 Jan. Cooperation North/Everyman Studio presents *The Midnight Court* in the Cork Arts and Theatre Club.

1990   24 Mar. Ray McBride performs *The Midnight Court* as part of Cúirt Literary Festival at Drimcong House, Moycullen (Galway).

1990   O'Brien Press (Dublin) reissues *The Midnight Court*, O'Connor's 1945 version. 72p. Awarded the silver medal by Irish publishers in annual Irish Book Awards for "imaginative reprinting."

1990   Mercier Press (Cork) reissues *The Midnight Court*, Patrick C. Power's bilingual version, fourth edition. 96p.

1990   Irish & Celtic Publications (Cork) publishes Dónal Ó Siodhacháin's edited volume, *The Midnight Court: Traditional Gaelic Burlesque Poem by Brian Merriman;* translated into English by Dennis Woulfe.

Publication/Production History

1991   Nora Relihan performs a one-woman show, *The Midnight Court* at Listowel Writers' Week (Kerry) and subsequently tours Ireland. Directed by Barry Cassin.

1992   Lisgold Productions produces *The Midnight Court* at the Dublin Theatre Festival (Andrews Lane).

1992   Druid Theatre Company (Galway) combines with Aeval Productions to produce *The Midnight Court,* Seán Tyrell's musical adaptation of David Marcus's English translation. Directed by Maelíosa Stafford. Cast includes Seán Keane, Mary McPartlan, and Seán Tyrell. Set design by Monica Frawley. Tours widely.

1992   Oct. Nora Relihan performs *The Midnight Court,* a one-woman show at Andrews Lane Theatre (Dublin) as part of Dublin Theatre Festival. Directed by Barry Cassin.

1994   June. Long Walk Music produces *The Midnight Court* at the Olympia Theatre (Dublin).

1997   Ben Gibney produces *The Midnight Court* as a screenplay for Irish Traditional Opera.

1998   Noel Fahey develops a website dedicated to the poem and its author.

1999   Nov. The Abbey Theatre tours Ireland with Tom MacIntyre's Irish-language dramatization of *Cúirt an Mheán Oíche.* Cast includes Karen Ardiff, Barry Barnes, Brendan Conroy, Lesley Conroy, Peadar Cox, Fiona Cronin, Bríd Ní Neachtain, Ríonach Ní Néill, Síle Nic Chonaonaigh, Niall Ó Síoradáin, and Tomás Ó Súilleabháin. Directed by Michael Harding, costume design by Joanna Taylor, and music by Steve Wickham. Opens at Peacock (Dublin) on 16 Nov. for thirteen performances. Tours 19 Oct.–13 Nov.

1999   Cois Life (Dublin) publishes *Cúirt an Mheán Oíche,* Tom MacIntyre's play, in association with the Abbey Theatre and the *Abbey Theatre Playscript Series.*

Publication/Production History

1999 Mercier Press (Cork) reissues *The Midnight Court*, Patrick C. Power's bilingual edition. 96p. Fifth edition.

2000 Harmattan (Paris) publishes *Le Tribunal de Minuit*, a French verse adaptation by René Agostini. 65p.

2000 The Gallery Press (Oldcastle, County Meath) publishes *The Midnight Verdict*, a partial English verse translation by Seamus Heaney. 48p.

2000 Burren Productions stage Brian Merriman's *Midnight Court*, a dramatic version of the poem at the Complex Theater, Santa Monica Boulevard, California. Produced by Hugh O'Neil and directed by Dermot Petty.

2002 *The Aisling Magazine* (An Charraig, Mainistir, Inis Mór, Aran Islands), no. 30, publishes a "literal and otherwise unpublished translation" by David Sowby.

2003 Celia de Fréine wins Duais an Oireachtais do Dhráma Ilghníomh for her dramatic adaptation of *Cúirt an Mheán Oíche*.

2005 Ashfield Press (Dublin) publishes *Cúirt an Mheadhon Oidhche/The Midnight Court*. Yam Cashen's translation ("done into Dublin English"). 55p.

2005 TG4 broadcast *Cosc ar Ghnéas*, a documentary that examines the banning of O'Connor's 1945 translation.

2005 The Gallery Press (Oldcastle, County Meath) publishes *The Midnight Court*, Ciarán Carson's English verse translation. 62p. Limited to one thousand copies, seventy-five of which are signed by author.

2005 Liam Ó Dochartaigh produces a dramatic reading of the text. Cast includes Eoghan Ó hAnluain, Áine Ó Ceallaigh, Audrey Ní Fhearghail, Alan Titley, and Doireann Ní Bhriain. Directed by Darach Mac Con Iomaire and subsequently made available by Raidió na Gaeltachta/Cumann Merriman as *Cúirt an Mheon-Oíche* on a commercial CD.

Publication/Production History

2005   Unofficial copies of the Seán Ó Ceallaigh (1896–1994) recording made available to Clare schools with assistance of Clare County Library.

2005   *The Appeal of the Midnight Court*. Produced by Cathal Póirtéir for RTÉ, this bilingual radio documentary commemorates the two hundredth anniversary of Merriman's's death.

2005   Seán Tyrrell's *Midnight Court* tours Ireland featuring Debra Wallace, Bernie O'Mahoney, Tess Purcell, Judy McKeown, Willie Greene, and Liam Rellis (producer).

2005   11–18 June. Queen of Puddings Music Theater Company premieres its original production *The Midnight Court*, a new Canadian opera based on O'Connor's translation, at the Harbourfront Theatre Center, Toronto. Composer: Ana Sokolovic; libretto: Paul Bentley; soprano: Shannon Mercer; mezzo-soprano: Krisztina Szabó; baritone: Alexander Dobson; musical directors: Dáirine Ní Mheadhra and John Hess; design: Michael Gianfrancesco; director: Michael Cavanagh. Subsequently chosen by Toronto's critics as one of the top ten shows of 2005 in all genres by the *Globe and Mail*, the *Toronto Star*, and *Eye Weekly*.

2006   Wake Forest University Press (Winston-Salem, NC) publishes *The Midnight Court*, Ciarán Carson's English verse translation in the United States. Illustrations by Elizabeth Rivers. 63p.

2006   Queen of Pudding tours and performs *The Midnight Court* at the Linbury Theatre, Royal Opera House, Covent Garden (London).

2007   Pauline Bewick exhibits her "visual translation," eleven paintings of the text at the Shelbourne Hotel (Dublin) and Kenny's Gallery (Galway). Limited edition of 250 presentation sets, eleven signed and numbered prints

	in their own exclusive presentation box, handmade by Muckross House Bindery.
2007	The Gallery Press republishes Ciarán Carson's English verse translation. 62p.
2007	July. The Dublin Shakespeare Society produces a revised version of Celia de Fréine's 1982 translation and dramatization of Brian Merriman's *Midnight Court* as part of their centenary celebrations at Theatre 36 (Dublin). Cast includes Ben Mulhern and Sarah Byrne. Directed by Helen Byrne, codirected by Debbie O'Sullivan.
2008	Bewick's visual interpretation exhibits at Irish College (Paris).

Additional Reading

Aaronson, L. 1946. "The Midnight Court." *Irish Times,* 22 Aug., 7.

Acton, Charles. 1973. "The Merryman Tradition." *Irish Times,* 20 Aug., 10.

Agostini, René. 1996. "Le bâtard dans *The Midnight Court* de Brian Merriman." In *Théâtres du Monde,* vol. 6, *Théâtre et Société: La Famille en Question,* edited by Maurice Abiteboul. Avignon: Université d'Avignon, Institut de recherches internationales sur les arts du spectacle, Faculté des lettres et des sciences numaines.

———. 2009. "Le Tribunal de Minuit de Brian Merriman ou la théâtralité d'un texte intemporel." In *Autour du Texte Théâtral,* edited by Edoardo Esposito. Paris: Editions L'Harmattan.

Bairéad, Ciarán. 1946. "Cúirt an Mheadhon-Oidhche: An American Translation." *The Irish Book Lover* 30, no. 1:8–11.

Béaslaí, Piaras. 1962. "Can Books in English Be 'Irish'?" *Irish Independent,* 3 Jan., 10.

———. 1963. "Anomoly of Censorship of Irish Poem." *Irish Independent,* 27 Mar., 7.

Bitter, R. 1946. "The Midnight Court." *Irish Times,* 13 Sept., 7.

Blunden, Edmund Charles. 1945. "Merryman's Vision." *Times Literary Supplement,* 6 Oct., 476.

Boland, Eavan. 1967. "The Morning After." *Irish Times,* 7 Jan., 8.

Breathnach, P. A. 1982–83. "Irish Narrative Poetry after 1200 A.D." *Studia Hibernica* 22–23:7–20.

Additional Reading

Breathnach, R. A. 1956. "Ad *Cúirt an Mheadhoin Oidhche* ll.597–8." *Éigse: A Journal of Irish Studies* 8, no. 2:140–43.

Carson, Ciarán. 2005. *The Midnight Court*. Oldcastle, Co. Meath: Gallery Press.

———. 2005. "Touched by the Master." *The Guardian*, 4 June.

Carty, Ciarán. 1981. "Giving Tongue to Our Poetic Roots." *Sunday Independent*, 21 June, 16.

Clarke, Austin. 1927. "From the Gaelic." *Times Literary Supplement*, 27 Jan., 53.

———. 1946. "The Midnight Court: A Rhythmical Bacchanalia from the Irish of Bryan Merriman, Translated by Frank O'Connor." *Dublin Magazine*, n.s., 21, no. 1:53–56 (Jan.–Mar.).

———. 1949. "Sense and Satire." *Irish Times*, 17 Dec., 6.

———. 1953. "Spirit of Laughter." *Irish Times*, 27 June, 6.

———. 1963. "Savage the Poet: No Foolish Face." *Irish Press*, 26 Jan., 6.

———. 1967. "The Midnight Court Updated." *Irish Press*, 21 Jan., 10.

———. 1968. "Bards and Hermits." *Times Literary Supplement*, 29 Feb., 206.

Cole, F. M. 1946. "The Midnight Court." *Irish Times*, 8 Aug., 5.

Colgan, Gerry. 1989. "The Midnight Court." *Irish Times*, 29 June, 10.

———. 1992. "The Midnight Court." *Irish Times*, 15 Oct., 8.

———. 1994. "The Midnight Court." *Irish Times*, 8 June, 12.

Craig, Patricia. 1983. "The Native's Vision." *Times Literary Supplement*, 21 Oct., 1162.

Cronin, Anthony. 1961. "Irish Poetry and Life." *Times Literary Supplement*, 30 June, 395.

Crowley, Tony. 2005. *Wars of Words: The Politics of Language in Ireland 1537–2004*. Oxford: Oxford Univ. Press.

Cullen, L. M. 1993. "The Contemporary and Later Politics of *Caoineadh Airt Uí Laoire*." In *Eighteenth-Century Ireland/Iris an Dá Chultúr* 8:7–38.

De Barra, Séamus. 1996. "The Midnight Court." *Irish Times*, 15 Apr., 15.

Additional Reading

————. 1998–99. "An Chairt Bheathaisnéise ag Pilib Barún ar Bhrian 'Merriman' Mac Con Mara [1836]." *Studia Hibernica* 30:155–66.

Dixon, Stephen. 1992. "Amusing Satire Is Still Relevant." *Irish Independent,* 15 Oct., 12.

Downey, Alan. 1946. "The Midnight Court." *Irish Times,* 15 Aug., 3.

"Drory." 1946. "The Midnight Court." *Irish Times,* 9 Aug., 7.

Eglinton, John. 1905. "The Best Irish Poem." *Bards and Saints,* 44–55. Dublin: Maunsel and Co.

E. H. A. 1930. *"The Midnight Court* and *The Adventures of a Luckless Fellow:* Two Poems Translated from the Gaelic by Percy Arland Ussher." *Hermathena* 20, nos. 44–45:216.

Everett-Green, Robert. 2005. "The Muck of the Irish Set to Music." *Globe and Mail* (Canada), 11 June.

Eyres, Harry. 1987. "Fairies Hold Sway: Review of Midnight Court at Jacob Street Studio." *Times* (London), 5 Dec.

Faller, Kevin. 1967. "Merriman's Frolic." *Irish Independent,* 11 Feb., 10.

"Fiachra Eilgeach." 1946. "The Midnight Court." *Irish Times,* 9 Aug., 7.

————. 1946. "The Midnight Court." *Irish Times,* 12 Aug., 5.

Fridberg, Maurice. 1946. "The Midnight Court." *Irish Times,* 2 Aug., 7.

Greene, David. 1945. "An Irish Bacchanalia." *Irish Times,* 29 Sept., 2.

————. 1946. "The Midnight Court." *Irish Times,* 15 Aug., 3.

Gunn, Marion. 1984. *A Chomharsain Éistigí agus Amhráin eile as Co. an Chláir.* Baile Átha Cliath: An Clóchomhar Tta.

Hartnett, Michael. 1972. "Back to Court." *Irish Press,* 27 May, 10.

Harvey Jacob, J. F. 1946. "The Midnight Court." *Irish Times,* 12 Aug., 5.

Heaney, Seamus. 1995. "Orpheus in Ireland: Merriman's *The Midnight Court.*" *The Southern Review* 31, no. 3:786–806.

Hill, Ian. 1999. "Heaving Bosoms and Bottoms in Old Gaelic Romp." *Belfast News Letter,* 6 Nov., 11.

Hogan, James. 1946. "The Midnight Court." *Irish Times,* 20 July, 5.

————. 1946. "The Midnight Court." *Irish Times,* 2 Aug., 7.

————. 1946. "The Midnight Court." *Irish Times,* 9 Aug., 7.

Additional Reading

"J. B. D." 1946. "The Midnight Court." *Irish Times,* 30 Aug., 6.

"J. B. S." 1946. "The Midnight Court." *Irish Times,* 1 Aug., 5.

"J. C." 1912. "Cúirt an Mheadhon Oidhche." *Cork Historical and Archaeological Society Journal* 18, nos. 94–96:214.

"J. J. D." 1946. "The Midnight Court." *Irish Times,* 10 Aug., 6.

"J. L. B." 1945. "Review of Frank O'Connor's *The Midnight Court.*" *Irish Press,* 4 Oct., 2.

Kane, Archer. 1972. "*The Midnight Court* in Trinity College." *Irish Times,* 10 Aug., 10.

Keane, J. 1946. "The Midnight Court." *Irish Times,* 12 Aug., 5.

Kelly, Seamus. 1968. "'The Midnight Court' at the Gate." *Irish Times,* 4 June, 8.

"MacM, F." 1949. "*The Midnight Court* again." *Irish Press,* 25 Aug., 6.

Mac Maghnaus, Peadar. "Letters to Editor." *Irish Times,* 29 July, 7.

MacManus, Francis. 1964. "A Fine Irish Magazine (*Studia Hibernica*)." *Irish Press,* 19 Sept., 6.

Mac Mathghamhna, Brian. 1961. "Kings, Lords and Commons." *Irish Times,* 25 July, 5.

Maguire, Des. 1968. "Merriman and Pope's Encyclical." *Irish Press,* 18 Sept., 3.

Mahon, B. 1946. "The Midnight Court." *Irish Times,* 3 Aug., 7.

Martin, Augustine. 1968. "A Pallid Sitting of the Midnight Court (Gate Theatre)." *Irish Press,* 4 June, 4.

McAdoo, H. R. 1939. "Notes on the Midnight Court." *Éigse: A Journal of Irish Studies* 1, no. 3:167–72.

McMahon, B. 1946. "The Midnight Court." *Irish Times,* 27 July, 8.

Meehan, James A. 1946. "The Midnight Court." *Irish Times,* 20 Aug., 3.

———. 1946. "The Midnight Court." *Irish Times,* 25 Aug., 5.

Mercier, Vivian. 1956. "The Uneventful Event." *Irish Times,* 18 Feb., 6.

Meyerstein, E. H. W. 1947. "The Midnight Court, by Bryan Merryman, Translated by Frank O'Connor." *English* 6, no. 34:213

Morgain, James. 1946. "The Midnight Court." *Irish Times,* 17 Aug., 3.

Morgan, James. 1946. "The Midnight Court." *Irish Times,* 23 Aug., 7.

Morony, M. "Merriman Goes Boom-Boom." *Irish Independent,* 10 June, 4.

Morrison, Richard. 2006. "The Midnight Court." *Times* (London), 3 July.

Murphy, Colin. 2005. "The Court of Sexual Appeal." *The Village,* 2–8 Sept.

Murphy, Gerard. 1939. "Notes on Aisling Poetry." *Éigse: A Journal of Irish Studies* 1, no. 1:40–50.

Newman, W. A. 1963. "Talking Points." *Irish Press,* 30 July, 9.

Nic Pháidín, Caoilfhionn. 1978. "An Aoir i Litríocht na Gaeilge: Mion: Suirbhé." *Comhar* 37, no. 5:12–14.

Ó Beoláin, Art. 1985. "Brian Merriman." In *Merriman agus Filí Eile,* 7–23. Baile Átha Cliath: An Clóchomhar Tta.

O'Brien, Eugene. 2004. "'More than a Language . . . No More of a Language': Merriman, Heaney, and the Metamorphoses of Translation." *Irish University Review* 34, no. 2:277–90.

O'Brien, Patrick. "The Midnight Court." *Irish Times,* 23 Aug., 7.

Ó Broin, Tomás. 1963. "Twa Mariit Wemen." *Feasta,* July, 8.

Ó Cadhain, Máirtín. 1968. "Curamhír Phobal na Gaeilge." *Comhar* 27, no. 12:7–11.

Ó Cianáin, Cormac. 1985. "An Sagart agus Brian Merriman." *Comhar* 44, no. 1:14–17.

Ó Conchúir, Breandán. 2000. "Na cúirteanna éigse i gCúige Mumhan." In *Saoi na hÉigse: Aistí in Ómós do Sheán Ó Tuama,* edited by Pádraigín Riggs et al., 55–104. Baile Átha Cliath: An Clóchomhar Tta.

O'Connell, F. W. 1905. "Brian Merriman's *Midnight Court*" (as translated by Stern). *Hermathena* 13, nos. 30–31:525–30.

O'Connor, Frank. 1946. "Justice How Are You?" *Irish Times,* 17 July, 5.

———. 1946. "The Midnight Court." *Irish Times,* 29 July, 5.

———. 1946. "The Midnight Court." *Irish Times,* 2 Aug., 7.

———. 1946. "The Midnight Court." *Irish Times,* 10 Aug., 6.

———. 1968. "Preface to the Midnight Court." *Irish Press,* 13 Sept., 11.

Ó Cuinn, Coslett. 1982. "Merriman's Court." In *The Pleasures of Gaelic Poetry,* edited by Seán Mac Réamoinn, 11–26. London: Allen Lane.

Ó Cuív, Brian. 1952. *Parliament na mBan.* Baile Átha Cliath: Institiúid Ard-Léinn.

Additional Reading

———. 1965. "*Cúirt an Mheán Oíche le Brian Merriman*, curtha in eagar ag Daithí Ó hUaithne." *Éigse: A Journal of Irish Studies* 13, no. 1 79–80.

———. 1965–66. "Rialacha do Chúirt Éigse i gContae an Chláir." *Éigse: A Journal of Irish Studies* 2:216–18.

———. 1973. "*Cúirt an Mheán-Oíche: The Midnight Court*. Brian Merriman. Text and Translation by Patrick C. Power." *Éigse: A Journal of Irish Studies* 15, no. 2:170.

Ó Donnchadha, Tadhg. 1946. "The Midnight Court." *Irish Times*, 22 Aug., 7.

O'Donoghue, Bernard. 2006. "Hush, Slush and Spuds." *Times Literary Supplement*, 17 Feb., 30.

Ó Drisceoil, Proinsias. 2005. "Anáil na heagnaíochta ar *Cúirt an Mheán Oíche*." *Bliainiris*, 130–42.

Ó Fiannachta, Pádraig. 1982. "Litríocht an Chláir san Ochtú hAois Déag." In *Léas eile ar ár Litríocht*, 229–46. Maigh Nuad: An Sagart.

Ó Floinn, Criostóir. 1972. "Foilsíu na Gaeilge i mBéarla." *Irish Press*, 25 July, 13.

———. 1972. "Cúirt Éigse sa Phéacóg." *Irish Press*, 28 Nov., 9.

Ó hAodha, Micheál. 1994. *Siobhán: A Memoir of an Actress*. Dingle, Co. Kerry: Brandon Books.

Ó hÓgáin, Dáithí. 1980. "Na cúirteanna éigse: fianaise an bhéaloidis." *Comhar* 39, no. 3:19–21.

Ó Muirí, Damien. 2002. "An Cúlra Dlíthiúil leis an Bharántas." In *Téada Dúchais: Aistí in ómós don Ollamh Breandán Ó Madagáin*, edited by Máirtín Ó Briain and Pádraig Ó hÉalaí, 423–44. Indreabhán: Cló Iar-Chonnachta.

Ó Murchú, Liam P. 1977–78. "Dearbhaithe ó Chontae an Chláir." *Éigse: A Journal of Irish Studies* 17:237–64.

———. 1996. "The Midnight Court." *Irish Times*, 5 Apr., 13.

———. 2000. "Cúlra agus Múnla Liteartha do Chúirt Mherriman." In *Saoi na hÉigse: Aistí in Ómós do Sheán Ó Tuama*, edited by Pádraigín Riggs, et al. 169–95. Baile Átha Cliath: An Clóchomhar Tta.

Additional Reading

———. 2010. "Merriman's *Cúirt An Mheonoíche* and Eighteenth-Century Irish Verse." In *A Companion to Irish Literature,* edited by Julia M. Wright, 178–92. Chicester: John Wiley and Sons.

Ó Nualláin, Ciarán. 1946. "The Midnight Court." *Irish Times,* 9 Aug., 7.

O'Quinn, Q. 1946. "The Midnight Court." *Irish Times,* 3 Aug., 7.

O'Rowen, Hamilton. 1946. "The Midnight Court." *Irish Times,* 15 Aug., 3.

Ó Seaghdha, Barra. 2010–11. "A Gift of Tongues." *Dublin Review of Books* 16, accessed online.

O'Sheehan, J. 1946. "The Midnight Court." *Irish Times,* 13 Aug., 5.

O'Toole, Fintan. 1984. "Anodyne Erse." *Sunday Tribune,* 14 Oct.

Ó Tuama, Seán. 1964. "Cúirt an Mheán Oíche." *Studia Hibernica* 4:7–27.

———. 1951. "Cúirt an mheán-oíche agus na léirmheastóirí—Frank O'Connor go speisialta." *Cork University Record,* no. 21.

———. 1967. "Cúirt an Mheán-oíche agus na léirmheastóirí, duine amháin go speisialta!" *Feasta,* April, 19.

———. 1980. "Brian Merriman and His Court." *Irish Times,* 23 Aug., 9.

———. 1990. "Cúirt an Mheán Oíche." In *Cúirt, Tuath agus Bruachbhaile: Aistí agus Dréachtaí Liteartha,* 7–37. Baile Átha Cliath: An Clóchomhar.

———. 1995. "Love in Irish Folksong." In *Repossessions: Selected Essays on the Irish Literary Heritage,* 134–58. Cork: Cork Univ. Press.

Pyle, Fitzroy. 1946. "The Midnight Court." *Irish Times,* 24 Aug., 7.

———. 1946. "The Midnight Court." *Irish Times,* 26 Aug., 5.

———. 1946. "The Midnight Court." *Irish Times,* 27 Aug., 5.

Quinn, E. G. 1949. "Merriman (Brian) *Cúirt an Mheadhón Oidhche.* Nuadh-eagar ag Risteárd Ó Foghludha (Fiachra Éilgeach). Baile Átha Cliath, 1949, 10s 6d." *Hermathena* 73:92–93.

Roche, Dick. 1982. "A Timely Launch." *Irish Independent,* 29 Sept., 6.

Rosenstock, Gabriel. "Merriman Rides Again." *Irish Times,* 23 Oct., 14.

Rushe, Desmond. 1968. "Relied on a Revue Technique." *Irish Independent,* 4 June, 12.

Sealy, Douglas. 1986. "Out of Court." *Irish Times,* 1 Feb., 12.

"Seán an Chóta." 1946. "The Midnight Court." *Irish Times,* 11 Sept., 5.

Additional Reading

Service, Tom. 2006. "The Midnight Court Opera." *The Guardian*, 1 July.

Terauds, John. 2005. "Colour This Court Operatic." *Toronto Star*, 13 June.

Titley, Alan. 1989–90. "An Breithiúnas ar *Cúirt an Mheán-Oíche*." *Studia Hibernica* 25:105–33.

Ua Casaide, Seamus. 1911. "Fictitious Dates." *The Irish Book Lover* 3, no. 1:13.

———. 1911. "The Midnight Court," *The Irish Book Lover* 3, no. 3:33–35.

Ussher, Arland. 1946. "The Midnight Court." *Irish Times*, 12 Sept., 7.

Vendryes, J. 1913. "*Cúirt an Mheadhon Oidhche*, Bryan Merryman cct, Risteárd Ó Foghludha .i. Fiachra Eilgeach do chuir in eagar." *Revue Celtique* 34:462–64.

Wheatley, David. 2005. "Fairies and Bondage Fantasies." *The Guardian*, 10 Sept.

"W. H. G. F." 1911. "The Midnight Court." *The Irish Book Lover* 3, no. 4:60–61.

Williams, Nicholas. 1977. "An Gháirsiúl i Litríocht na Gaeilge." *Comhar* 37, no. 4:13–16, and 37, no. 6:8–12.

"W. P. M." 1953. "Review of *The Midnight Court*, Translated by David Marcus." *Dublin Magazine*, n.s., 28, no. 4:51.

———. 1901. "Review of Rev. Canon F. W. O'Connell's Book." *Freeman's Journal*, 24 July, 5.

———. 1909. "Merriman." In *The Dictionary of National Bibliography* 13, edited by Sidney Lee, 292. London: Macmillan Company.

———. 1910. "Vision of Female Judgment." *Irish Independent*, 14 Mar., 7.

———. 1910. "An Irish Poet-Satirist." *Irish Independent*, 11 Nov., 7.

———. 1913. "Review: The Midnight Court." *Irish Times*, 24 Jan.

———. 1926. "An Irish Rabelais." *Irish Times*, 1 Oct., 3.

———. 1946. "Banned Books." *Irish Times*, 18 May, 4.

———. 1946. "An Irishman's Diary." *Irish Times*, 16 July, 5.

———. 1946. "Gaelic Books." *Irish Times*, 20 July, 4.

———. 1946. "Justice How Are You?" *Irish Times*, 20 July, 5.

———. 1946. "Editorial." *Irish Times*, 23 Aug., 5.

Additional Reading

———. 1946. "Regulations on Censorship of Publications." *Irish Times,* 30 Aug., 7.

———. 1946. "Brian Merriman Memorial." *Irish Press,* 21 Nov., 7.

———. 1949. "The Midnight Court Translated by Lord Longford from the Irish of Bryan Merriman." Introduction by Padraic Colum. *Poetry Ireland* 6.

———. 1956. "Radio Review." *Irish Times,* 2 Nov., 8.

———. 1957. "Bilingual Frolic for Tóstal." *Irish Times,* 22 May, 4.

———. 1961. "Ban on Frank O'Connor's Book Lifted." *Irish Times,* 9 Dec., 13–14.

———. 1972. "Court at TCD Is Rewarding." *Irish Press,* 9 Aug., 4.

Internet resources

Cúirt an Mheadhon-Oidhche–The Midnight Court, Noel Fahey's Web site dedicated to the poem; includes text in Irish and English, http://www.showhouse.com.

Cumann Merriman website; the Merriman Winter and Summer school with biographical and cultural information. http://www.merriman.ie/merriman/index.en.

Kenny Gallery, The Visual Translation of *The Midnight Court,* Pauline Bewick's visual interpretation of the poem, http://www.thekennygallery.ie/exhibitions/2007/bewickpauline.

References

Bakhtin, M. M. 1981. *The Dialogic Imagination: Four Essays.* Edited by Michael Holquist; translated by Caryl Emerson and Michael Holquist. Austin: Univ. of Texas Press.

Béaslaí, Piaras. 1912. "Merriman's Secret: An Interpretation." In *Cúirt an Mheadhon Oidhche,* edited by Ristéard Ó Foghludha, 1–19. Dublin: Hodges, Figgis and Co.

Bogel, Fredric V. 2001. *The Difference Satire Makes: Rhetoric and Reading from Jonson to Byron.* Ithaca: Cornell Univ. Press.

Buttimer, Neil. 2006. "Literature in Irish, 1690–1800: From the Williamite Wars to the Act of Union." In *The Cambridge History of Irish Literature,* edited by Margaret Kelleher and Philip O'Leary, vol. 1, 320–71. Cambridge: Cambridge Univ. Press.

Caerwyn Williams, J. E., and Máirín Ní Mhuiríosa. 1979. *Traidisiún Liteartha na nGael.* Baile Átha Cliath: An Clóchomhar Tta.

Carson, Ciarán. 2005. "Introduction." In *The Midnight Court.* Oldcastle, Co. Meath: The Gallery Press.

———. 2009. "The Thing Itself." *Journal of Music in Ireland* Jan./Feb., accessed 1 Mar. 2010, http://journalofmusic.com/article/901.

Corkery, Daniel. 2004. *The Hidden Ireland: A Study of Gaelic Munster Poetry in the Eighteenth Century.* Eugene, OR: Wipf and Stock Publishers (1924; previously published by Gill and Macmillan, 1967).

Croghan, Martin J. 1995. "Female Sexuality in *The Midnight Court* and *Ulysses.*" In *Troubled Histories, Troubled Fictions: Twentieth Century*

References

Anglo-Irish Prose, edited by Theo D'haen and José Lanters, 19–30. Amsterdam: Rodopi.

Cullen, Louis. 1996. "Filíocht, cultúr agus polaitíocht." In *Nua-Léamha: Gnéithe de Chultúr, Stair agus Polaitíocht na hÉireann c. 1600–c. 1900*, edited by Máirín Ní Dhonnchadha, 170–99. Baile Átha Cliath: An Clóchomhar Tta.

Cullingford, Elizabeth Butler. 1994. "Pornography and Canonicity: The Case of Yeats's 'Leda and the Swan.'" In *Representing Women: Law, Literature and Feminism*, edited by Susan Sage Heinzelman and Zipporah Batshaw Wiseman, 165–88. Duke: Duke Univ. Press.

de Blacam, Aodh. 1935. *A First Book of Irish Literature*. Dublin: The Talbot Press.

de Paor, Liam. 1988. "Introduction." In *Tomás Ó Míocháin, Filíocht*, edited by Diarmuid Ó Muirithe, 10–32. Baile Átha Cliath: An Clóchomhar Tta.

———. 1998. "The World of Brian Merriman: County Clare in 1780." In *Landscape with Figures: People, Culture, and Art in Ireland and the Modern World*, edited by Liam de Paor, 37–64. Dublin: Four Courts.

Dickson, David. 2005. *Old World Colony: Cork and South West Munster 1630–1830*. Cork: Cork Univ. Press.

Everett-Green, Robert. 2005. "The Magic of a Midsummer's Nightmare." *Globe and Mail* (Canada), 13 June.

Falk, Robert P., and Frances Teague. 1993. "Parody." In *The New Princeton Encyclopedia of Poetry and Poetics*, edited by Alex Preminger et al., 881. Princeton: Princeton Univ. Press.

Fitzgerald, D. J. L. (P. M. F.). 1945. "Mr. O'Connor in Fairyland." *Punch* 209, no. 5470:406–7.

Gaelic League. n.d.a. "The Irish Language and Irish Intermediate Education." Pamphlet no. 6. Gaelic League Pamphlets. Dublin: Gaelic League Publications.

———. n.d.b. "The Irish Language and Irish Intermediate Education: Dr. Hyde's Reply to Dr. Atkinson." Gaelic League Pamphlets. Dublin: Gaelic League Publications.

References

————. n.d.c. "The Irish Language and Irish Intermediate Education."
Pamphlet no. 9. Gaelic League Pamphlets. Dublin: Gaelic League
Publications.

Greeley, Andrew M. 1980. "The American Achievement: A Report from
Great Ireland." In *America and Ireland, 1776–1976: The American
Identity and the Irish Condition,* edited by David N. Doyle and Owen
D. Edwards, 231–46. Westport, CT: Greenwood.

Heaney, Seamus. 1995. "Orpheus in Ireland: On Brian Merriman's *The
Midnight Court.*" In *The Redress of Poetry,* 38–62. New York: Noon-
day Press.

Heffernan, James A. W. 2004. "Joyce's Merrimanic Heroine: Molly vs.
Bloom in Midnight Court." *James Joyce Quarterly* 41, no. 4:745–66.

Hull, Eleanor. 1913. *Textbook of Irish Literature.* Part 2. Dublin: M. N.
Gill and Son.

Hyde, Douglas. n.d. *A University Scandal.* Dublin: Gaelic League
Publications.

Jackson, Mark. 1996. *New-Born Murder: Women, Illegitimacy and the
Courts in Eighteenth-Century England.* Manchester: Manchester
Univ. Press.

Kellaway, Kate. 1995. "An Irishman Doing English." *The Observer,* 10 Sept.

Kelly, Liam. 1996. "Vicar Raps Booze Play." *Daily Mirror,* 29 Mar., 8.

Kenrick, W. 1794. *The Whole Duty of Woman: Or, A Complete System of
Female Morality.* London: J. Wallis, No. 16, Ludgate-street.

Kiberd, Declan. 2000. "Brian Merriman's Midnight Court." In *Irish Clas-
sics,* 182–202. London: Granta.

Lloyd, John. 1986. *Lloyd's Tour of Clare 1780, from Henn's Exact Reprint
of 1893.* Whitegate: Ballinakella Press.

MacKillop, James. 1998. *Dictionary of Celtic Mythology.* New York: Oxford
Univ. Press.

Macrae, Alasdair. 1993. "Poet Finds That Life at Its Best Is Never Immac-
ulate." *Herald* (Glasgow), 28 Apr.

Marcus, David. 1989. "Introduction." In *The Midnight Court and Other
Poems Translated from the Irish.* Dublin: Poolbeg.

References

McCormack, W. J. 1994. *From Burke to Beckett: Ascendancy, Tradition and Betrayal in Literary History.* Cork: Cork Univ. Press.

Mokyr, Joel, and Cormac Ó Grada. 1984. "New Developments in Irish Population History, 1700–1850." *Economic History Review,* n.s., 37, no. 4:473–88.

Morley, Vincent. 2002. *Irish Opinion and the American Revolution, 1760–1783.* Cambridge: Cambridge Univ. Press.

———. 2005. *Washington i gCeannas a Ríochta: Cogadh Mheiriceá i Litríocht na Gaeilge.* Baile Átha Cliath: Coiscéim.

Ní Chuilleanáin, Eiléan. 2005. "Mirror on a Classic." *Irish Times,* 30 July, C13.

Ní Mhuirgheasa, Máirín. 1951. "Cúirt an Mheán-Oíche agus Finnscéal an Róis." *Feasta,* May, 7.

Ó Buachalla, Breandán. 1996. *Aisling Ghéar: Na Stíobhartaigh agus an tAos Léinn 1603–1788.* Baile Átha Cliath: An Clóchomhar Tta.

———. 2005. "Cúirt an Mheon-Oíche by Brian Merriman." Unpublished typescript of lecture delivered by the late Breandán Ó Buachalla. Copy in possession of editor.

Ó Casaide, Séamus. 1937. "Poet Philomath and Flax Sower." *The Irish Book Lover* 25, nos. 4–6:103.

O'Connor, Frank. 1945. "Preface." In *The Midnight Court: A Rhythmical Bacchanalia from the Irish of Bryan Merryman.* Dublin: Maurice Fridberg.

———. 1970. "Introduction." In *Kings, Lords and Commons: An Anthology from the Irish,* vii–xv. Dublin: Gill and Macmillan.

Ó Crualaoich, Gearóid. 1983. "The Vision of Liberation in Cúirt an Mheán Oíche." In *Folia Gadelica: Essays Presented to R. A. Breathnach,* edited by Pádraig de Brún et al., 95–104. Cork: Cork Univ. Press.

———. 2003. *The Book of the Cailleach: Stories of the Wise-Woman Healer.* Cork: Cork Univ. Press.

Ó Cuív, Brian. 1986. "Irish Language and Literature, 1691–1845." In *A New History of Ireland,* vol. 4., edited by T. W. Moody and W. E. Vaughan, 374–423. Oxford: Clarendon Press.

References

Ó Dálaigh, Brian. 1993. "Tomás Ó Míocháin and the Ennis School of Gaelic Poetry c. 1730–1804." *Dal gCais: The Journal of Clare*, 2:55–73.

———. 2000. "'Poet of a Single Poem,' Brian Merriman (c. 1749–1805)." In *County Clare Studies: Essays in Memory of Gerald O'Connell, Seán Ó Murchadha, Thomas Coffey, and Pat Flynn*, edited by Ciarán Ó Murchadha, 101–36. Ennis: Clare Archaeological and Historical Society.

O'D(onoghue), D. J. 1911. "Brian Merriman." *The Irish Book Lover* 3, no. 2:31.

Ó Fiannachta, Pádraig. 1978. *An Barántas*. Maigh Nuad: An Sagart.

———. 1991. "The Poetic Warrant." *Studia Celtica Japonica* 4:1–13.

———. 1982. "Litríocht an Chláir san Ochtú hAois Déag." In *Léas eile ar ár Litríocht*, edited by Pádraig Ó Fiannachta, 229–46. Maigh Nuad: An Sagart.

O'Flaherty, Gerard. 1967. "The Midnight Court by Bryan Merriman. Translated into English by David Marcus. Dolmen Press. 9s. 6d." *Dublin Magazine* 6, no. 1:100–101.

Ó Foghludha, Ristéard. 1949. "Brian Merriman: Beatha an fhile." *Cúirt an Mheadhón Oidhche*, 7–13. Baile Átha Cliath: Hodges, Figgis and Co.

Ó Glaisne, Risteárd. 1996. *Coslett Ó Cuinn*. Baile Átha Cliath: Coiscéim.

Ó hAnluain, Eoghan. 2000. "Cuirfidh mé faghairt i bhfeidhm más cruaidh dom. Draíocht chun drúise in *Cúirt an Mheon-Oíche*." In *Saoi na hÉigse: Aistí in Ómós do Sheán Ó Tuama*, edited by Pádraigín Riggs, et al., 153–67. Baile Átha Cliath: An Clóchomhar Tta.

Ó hÓgáin, Daithí. 1991. *Myth, Legend and Romance: An Encyclopaedia of the Irish Folk Tradition*. New York: Prentice Hall Press.

Ó Muirithe, Diarmuid. 1988. *Tomás Ó Míocháin: Filíocht*. Baile Átha Cliath: An Clóchomhar Tta.

Ó Murchú, Liam P. 1982. *Cúirt an Mheon-Oíche le Brian Merríman*. Baile Átha Cliath: An Clóchomhar Tta.

———. 2005. *Merriman: I bhFábhar Béithe*. Baile Átha Cliath: An Clóchomhar Tta.

O'Neill, Kevin. 1984. "A Demographer Looks at *Cúirt an Mheán-Oíche*." *Éire-Ireland* 19, no. 2:135–43.

References

O'Rahilly, T. F. 1912. "Review." *Gadelica* no. 1:190–204.

———. 1926. *Dánta Grádha*. Cork: Cork Univ. Press.

Ó Tuama, Seán. 1981. "Brian Merriman and His Court." In *Irish University Review* 11, no. 2:149–64.

———. 1995. "Brian Merriman and His Court." In *Repossessions: Selected Essays on the Irish Literary Heritage*, 63–77. Cork: Cork Univ. Press.

Ó Tuathaigh, Gearóid. 1978. "The Role of Women in Ireland under the New English Order." In *Women in Irish Society: The Historical Dimension*, edited by Margaret McCurtain and Donncha Ó Corráin, 26–36. Dublin: Arlen House.

Perrin, J. M. 1956. *Virginity*. Translated by Katherine Gordon. London: Blackfriars Publications.

Power, Patrick C. 1990. "Introduction." In *The Midnight Court*, 6–12. Cork: Mercier Press.

Terry, Richard. 1992. "Transitions and Digressions in the Eighteenth-Century Long Poem." *Studies in English Literature, 1500–1900* 32, no. 3:496.

Tymoczko, Maria. 1994. *The Irish Ulysses*. Berkeley: Univ. of California Press.

Welch, Robert, ed. 1996. *The Oxford Companion to Irish Literature*, Oxford: Clarendon Press.

Yeats, W. B. 1926. Introduction to *The Midnight Court* and *The Adventures of a Luckless Fellow*, edited by Percy Arland Ussher, 5–12. London: Jonathan Cape.

———. 1980. "Merriman Poem Sexist Rubbish." *Irish Times*, 29 Aug., 11.

———. 1996. "Good Friday Show a Hit." *Sunday Independent*, 7 Apr., 2.

Biographical Notes

Brian Merriman

(c. 1749–1805)

Other than the date of Merriman's death, little can be stated with certainty regarding the poet's life. Merriman was born at Ennistymon about 1749. His mother was Quilkeen, but controversy surrounds his father's identity—he was possibly a priest or a stone mason commissioned to erect the Deerpark walls at Ennistymon—and when exactly, or if, they married. For reasons unknown—possibly on account of his (step)father gaining employment in nearby Caher—the family relocated to Lough Graney, near Killanena, Feakle, where Merriman spent his childhood. Little is known of his formal education, either. Somewhere around 1787 he married Kathleen Collins (born approx. 1767) from Feakle, with whom he had two daughters: Máire (born 1790) and Caitlín (born 1795). Merriman farmed a twenty-acre holding near Lough Graney in addition to teaching in nearby Kilclaren. In the year 1796, to encourage the growth of flax and hemp seed, the Board of Trustees of the Linen and Hempen Manufacturers of Ireland, founded in 1782, awarded spinning wheels, reels, or looms, in proportion to the acreage sown. "To the person who should sow between the 10th day of March and the 1st day of June 1796 with a sufficient quantity of good sound flax-seed, any quantity of land, well prepared and fit for the purpose not less than 1 Acre—4 Spinning Wheels, 3 Roods—3 ditto, 2 Roods—2 ditto and 1 Rood—1 ditto. And to the person who should sow in like manner any quantity of like land, not less than 5 Acres, a loom or

Biographical Notes

Brian Merriman [signature]

From a print in 'Irishman' newspaper, 1880.

Brian Merriman. From the *Irishman*, 1880.

wheels, reels or hatchells to the value of 50 shillings, and for every 5 Acres over and above the first 5, a like premium." While most activity was in Ulster, the 1796 Spinning Wheel/Flax Growers Bounty list notes approximately 60,000 names nationwide and approximately 178 flax farmers in County Clare. Among the five farmers listed for Fealke is Brian Merryman, who received two wheels (Ó Casaide 1937, 103). Merriman/Merrymans are also listed in Louth, Roscommon and Westmeath. About 1802 Merriman moved his family to Limerick city, where he established a school and continued to teach. The school was situated at 74/5 Clare Street, while the family resided on nearby Old Clare Street. His death on 27 July 1805 was announced two days later in the *General Advertiser and Limerick Gazette*:

Biographical Notes

"Died: on Saturday morning in Old Clare-street, after a few hours' illness, Mr. Bryan Merriman, teacher of mathematics, etc." The following Thursday, *Faulkner's Dublin Journal* also reported his demise as follows: "At Limerick, after a few hours illness, Mr. Bryan Merryman, teacher of mathematics." *Walker's Hibernian Magazine* (August) also recorded his death. The poet is buried in an unmarked grave in Feakle cemetery, where a plaque now honors his memory. Máire, his elder daughter, married Andrew Bolger, a tailor, circa 1814 and moved to London after her father's death where they raised two daughters, Máire and Nora, at 6 Denzel Street, now Kingsway, London. Bolger subsequently altered his name to Butler. Caitlín also married a tailor, Michael Ryan, and they lived at 45 Mary's Street in Limerick city, not far from the family home. They had two sons, Seán and Brian (Ó Foghludha 1949).

David Marcus
(1924–2009)

The grandson of a Jewish refugee from Lithuania, David Marcus was born in Cork City, Ireland, 21 August 1924. He received his formal education at Presentation Brothers; University College, Cork; and King's Inns, Dublin. Called to the bar in 1945, he practiced law for several years in Dublin. In 1946, in tandem with Terence Smith, he founded the periodical *Irish Writing*, which he edited until 1954. In 1948 he established the journal *Poetry Ireland* and acted as its editor until 1954. He sold the journal in 1955 and moved to London, where he worked in the insurance business before returning to Ireland in 1967 to work for the *Irish Press*. As the paper's literary editor from April 1968 to 1986, he established the highly influential "New Irish Writing" page that served as an important forum for many emerging writers of both English and Irish. In 1976 he assisted Philip McDermott in establishing the Poolbeg Press. On retiring from the *Irish Press* in 1986 to focus on his own creative writing, he was widely acknowledged as a pivotal figure in Irish literary circles who influenced many modern Irish writers. In addition to more than thirty edited volumes of Irish short stories and poetry,

Biographical Notes

David Marcus. Courtesy of Ita Daly.

the most recent of which was *The Faber Book of Best New Irish Short Stories* (2007), he authored several novels, a collection of short stories, and a collection of poetry. Among his publication are *Six Poems* (1952), *To Next Year in Jerusalem* (1954), *A Land Not Theirs* (1986), *A Land in Flames* (1987), and *Who Ever Heard of an Irish Jew? and Other Stories* (1988). He also penned two autobiographical volumes: *Oughtobiography: Leaves from the Diary of a Hyphenated Jew* (2001) and *Buried Memories* (2004). He received the Rooney prize in 2001 for services to Irish literature and an honorary doctorate from University College, Cork, in 2005. David Marcus died 9 May 2009.

Biographical Notes

Contributors

Michael Griffin lectures in English studies at the University of Limerick. He has published widely in eighteenth-century and Irish studies in journals such as the *Review of English Studies, Eighteenth-Century Ireland, Field Day Review,* and *Utopian Studies.* He directed the 2006 Merriman Summer School.

Sarah E. McKibben is associate professor of Irish language and literature at the University of Notre Dame, where she has taught since 2002. Her publications include essays in *Blackwell's Companion to Irish Literature, Éire-Ireland, Proceedings of the Harvard Celtic Colloquium, The Irish Review,* and *Research in African Literatures.* Her book on early modern Irish-language poetry, *Endangered Masculinities in Irish Poetry, 1540–1780,* appeared in 2010.

Bríona Nic Dhiarmada is the Notre Dame chair of Irish language and literature and concurrent professor of film, television and theater studies at the University of Notre Dame. She is the author of *Téacs Baineann, Téacs Mná,* a full-length study on the poetry of Nuala Ní Dhomhnaill, which won Merriman Book of the Year (2006). She was a contributor to the *Cambridge History of Irish Literature* (2006) and a contributing editor to volume 5 of the *Field Day Anthology of Irish Writing* as well as co-editor (with Máire Ní Annracháin) of *Téacs agus Comhthéacs* (1998). She continues to direct Irish-language documentaries, the latest of which, *Ar Lorg Shorcha/ Searching for Sorcha,* won the 2007 Oireachtas prize.

Brian Ó Conchubhair is associate professor of Irish language and literature at the University of Notre Dame and a fellow of the Keough-Naughton Institute for Irish Studies. His publications include *Fin de siècle na Gaeilge: Darwin, an athbheochan agus smaointeoireacht na hEorpa* (2009), *Why Irish? The Irish Language and Literature in Academia* (2008), and *Gearrscéalta ár Linne* (2006). He also edited *Dublin's Fighting Story, 1916–1921* (2009),

Biographical Notes

Limerick's Fighting Story, 1916–1921 (2009), *Rebel Cork's Fighting Story, 1916–1921* (2009), and *Kerry's Fighting Story, 1916–1921* (2009).

Alan Titley is professor of modern Irish at University College Cork since 2006. His publications include *Máirtín Ó Cadhain: Clár Saothair* (1975), *An tÚrscéal Gaeilge* (1991), *Chun Doirne: Rogha Aistí* (1996), *A Pocket Book of Gaelic Culture* (2000), *Beir leat do Shár-Ghaeilge!* (2004), and *Scríbhneoirí faoi Chaibidil* (2010). In addition to his scholarship, he is an *Irish Times* columnist, novelist, short story and fable writer, broadcaster, and playwright.

Index

145

Index

Index

Index

Index

Index

Index

Index